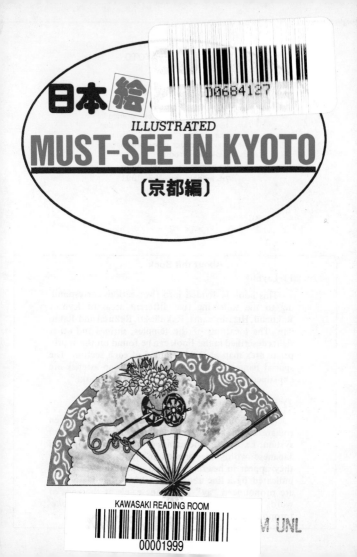

日本 絵

ILLUSTRATED

MUST-SEE IN KYOTO

（京都編）

ILLUSTRATED
MUST-SEE IN KYOTO

1st edition·········Sep., 1985
7th edition·········Nov., 1991
Printed in Japan

About this Book

1) Layout

This book is divided into five sections correspond-
ing to the following five different areas of Kyōto:
Rakuchū, Higashi-yama, Rakuhoku, Rakusai and Rakunan. The locations of the temples, shrines and other
sights described in the book can be found on the appro-
priate area map at the beginning of each section. The
special names and terms marked with an asterisk are
explained in the glossary at the end of the book.

2) Japanese Words

All the Japanese words in this book have been
romanized in accordance with the revised Hepburn
system. Except for the names of places and people, all
Japanese words are printed in italics except where
they appear in headings or bold type. Long vowels are
indicated by a line above, as in *'shintō'*; and, since e's
are pronounced "ay" in Japanese, e's at the ends of
words are marked with an acute accent, as in *'saké'*
(pronounced "sahkay").

Dear Readers

Almost twelve hundred years have passed since the first Imperial Palace was built at Kyōto in A.D. 794 and the city became the capital of Japan. Kyōto's economic and political influence has waxed and waned through the ages, but it has always been one of Japan's most important political, economic and cultural centers, and the driving-force behind much of the country's history. Kyōto's history and culture could without exaggeration be said to be the history and culture of Japan itself.

This book is an informative, easily-read guide which makes liberal use of illustrations to introduce the beautiful ancient capital that is Kyōto. To visit Kyōto is to discover that the time-honored traditions of Japan still live on. We hope that this book will help to make your visit even more rewarding and enjoyable.

Some of the places introduced in this book requre reservations, and special permission is needed to visit some of the temples and shrines. For detailed information, contact the Japan National Tourist Organization TIC Kyoto, Phone (075)371-5649.

For words or items marked with *, see GLOSSARY starting on p. 176 for detailed descriptions.

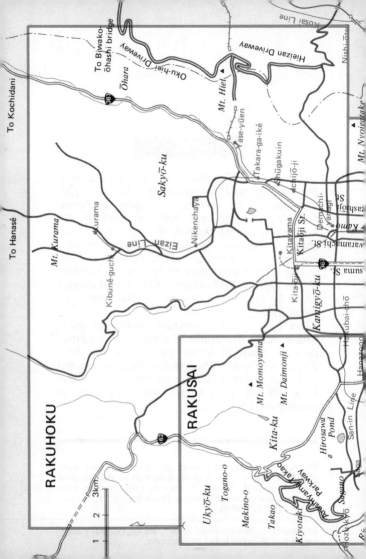

CONTENTS

✿

RAKUHOKU

RAKUSAI

RAKUNAN

Key to Symbols

 Temples

 Shrines, palaces, and buildings other than temples

 Shopping and sightseeing areas

 Festivals and performing arts

Food and traditional arts and crafts

Other

SEE KYŌTO WITH JTB'S SUNRISE TOURS

The Japan Travel Bureau's Sunrise Tours were specially developed with the foreign visitor in mind. Tours lasting from one day to two weeks are available to all the most interesting parts of Japan. The following are including Kyōto.

Round Trip from Tōkyō

*Sunrise Express to Kyōto (1 day)
Sanjūsangendō Hall, Heian Shrine, Kiyomizu Temple
¥46,500

*Sunrise Express to Kyoto & Nara (2 days)
Day 1: Nara
Day 2: Nijō Castle, Old Imperial Palace Plaza, Golden Pavilion, Kyōto Handicraft Center, Sanjusangendo Hall, Heian Shrine, Kiyomizu Temple ¥65,000

One Way from Tōkyō to Kyōto

*Sunrise Holiday to Hakone & Kyōto (2 days)
Day 1: Hakone
Day 2: Nijō Castle, Old Imperial Palace Plaza, Golden Pavilion, Kyōto Handicraft Center ¥49,200

City Tour in Kyōto

*Kyōto Morning Tour
Departure: 9:00 a.m.
Nijō Castle, Old Imperial Palace Plaza, Golden Pavilion, Kyōto Handicraft Center
¥5,000

*Kyōto Afternoon Tour
Departure: 2:00 p.m.
Sanjūsangendō Hall, Heian Shrine, Kiyomizu Temple
¥5,000

*Kyōto Special Night Tour
Departure: 6:40 p.m.
Tea ceremony and Tempura dinner in a Japanese inn, Japanese traditional arts at Gion Corner
¥9,500

Notes   *Tours depart every day.

*Pickup and sending services are available from/to major hotels.

*The above prices are adults' prices for standard tours. Deluxe tours are also available at special prices.

*For bookings and information, contact:
Tōkyō (03)3276-7777
Kyōto (075)341-1413

Rakuchū, the city center,
is the site of many huge temples and palaces.
To walk through its streets is to see
the thousand-year history of Kyōto
unfold before one's eyes.

RAKUCHŪ

Kyōto prefecture

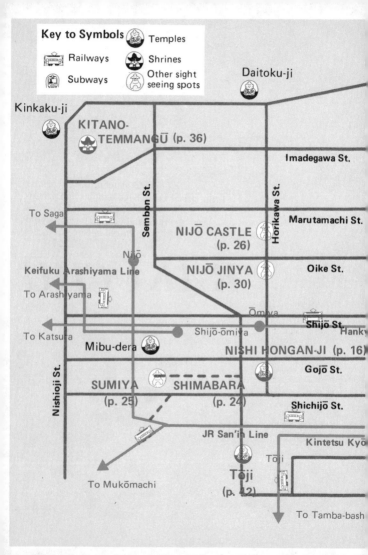

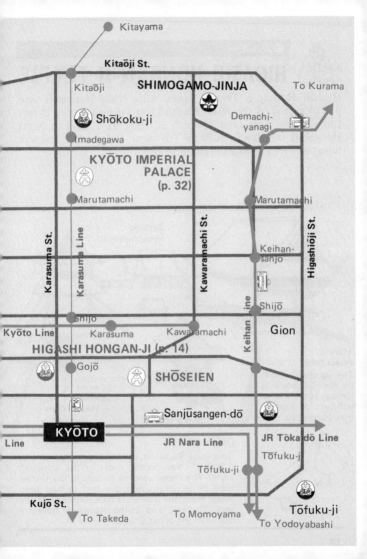

HIGASHI HONGAN-JI TEMPLE

Higashi Hongan-ji Temple ranks with Nishi Hongan-ji (see p. 16) as one of the *Jōdo-shinshū** sect's main temples. It was founded by Tokugawa Ieyasu* in 1602 as a rival to Nishi Hongan-ji, which was built by Toyotomi Hideyoshi*; and was burnt down in 1864 and rebuilt in 1895.

Settaijo (reception hall)

Hondō (main hall)

The square in front of the Taishi-dō is famous for the large numbers of pigeons that congregate there.

Taishidō Gate

Information Center

Hondō Gate

Shōrō (belfry)

Daishi-dō

This huge Buddhist hall, occupying an area of 3,900 m², has double roofs in the *Irimoya** style. The ropes used to transport the timber used in its construction are said to have been made from the hair of female followers of the sect. The hall is so called because it houses a statue of the priest Shinran*.

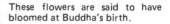

These flowers are said to have bloomed at Buddha's birth.

Shōsei Garden

This garden to the east of the temple, also called Kikoku Garden because of the hedge of *kikoku* (trifoliate orange) that surrounds it, was completed in 1657. It is landscaped in the go-round style, with various buildings arranged around a central lake, the Ingetsu Pond. It has the Thirteen Beautiful Landscapes (*Jūsan-kei*) featured in many *tanka** poems.

NISHI HONGAN-JI TEMPLE

Nishi Hongan-ji is the main temple of the *Jōdo-shinshū** Hongan-ji sect. It was founded in 1272 and moved to its present site in 1591 by Toyotomi Hideyoshi*. It features five buildings designated as national treasures besides a large number of beautiful works of art and is famous for its many examples of the showy and gorgeous artistic style of the Momoyama Era*.

The openwork carvings on the sides of the gate depict ancient Chinese historical events.

The carvings-in-the-round on the front of the gate show mainly *kara-jishi* (Chinese lions).

This magnificent 4-legged gate features a roof in the *Irimoya** style with a *Kara-hafu** decorated with brilliantly-colored ornamental carvings.

Irimoya-styled roof

Kara-hafu

Kara-mon (Chinese Gate)

This gate is also known as Higurashi-mon (Sunset Gate), since it is held to be easy to become so absorbed in admiring its exquisite beauty that one fails even to notice that the sun has set.

Funa-iri — boats would be moored here and the building entered by a flight of steps.

The *Katō-mado* of the Hiun-kaku is covered with a fine lattice. The name *Katō-mado* derives from the flames like shape of this type of window, since *Katō* literally means "fire head".

Hiun-kaku stands in the center of the Sōrō Pond. At the time it was built, its only means of access was by boat.

Third story:
Hōgyō * roof style

Second story: *Kara-hafu* / *Yosémuné* * roof style

First story: *Kara-hafu* / *Irimoya** roof style

Ryūhai-kyō (Dragon's-back Bridge)
This is the longest stone bridge in Japan.

Hiun-kaku

This three-storied mansion standing in the Tekisui Garden in the south-east corner of the temple grounds is known for its delicate and complex structure consisting of a combination of three different architectural styles. It is one of the architectural masterpieces of the Momoyama Era.

The *shoin** at Hongan-ji is divided into two halls, called Taimen-jo and Shiro-shoin hall. Both of these large halls are excellent examples of the *shoin** architectural style.

Taimenjo (Audience room)

Chōdai gamaé
This secret chamber, also called *musha-kakushi* (hiding-place for soldiers), is hidden behind the *fusuma** at the back of the upper hall.

Chigai-dana
Staggered shelves
Katō-mado
A special kind of window characteristic of Buddhist architecture.

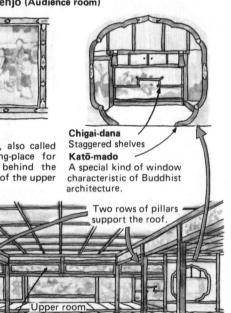

Two rows of pillars support the roof.

Upper room

Lower room

Open work screen

This huge hall, which has an area of 330 m², is used for audiences between the *monshu* (head priest) and his flock. The room is divided into two parts, an upper and a lower, with an openwork screen depicting *unchū-hikō* (swans in the clouds) above the division, from which the room derives its other name, Ōtori-no-ma (the Swan Room).

Shiro-Shoin

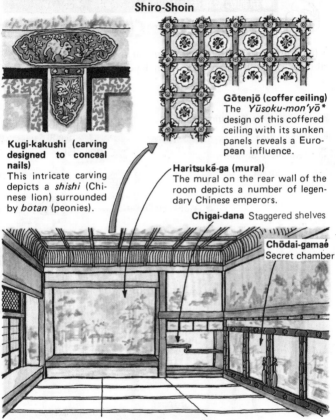

Kugi-kakushi (carving designed to conceal nails)
This intricate carving depicts a *shishi* (Chinese lion) surrounded by *botan* (peonies).

Gōtenjō (coffer ceiling)
The *Yūsoku-mon'yō* * design of this coffered ceiling with its sunken panels reveals a European influence.

Haritsuké-ga (mural)
The mural on the rear wall of the room depicts a number of legendary Chinese emperors.

Chigai-dana Staggered shelves

Chōdai-gamaé Secret chamber

Shimyō-no-ma

Shiro-Shoin has three chambers; Jōdan-no-ma (the first room), Ni-no-ma (the second room) and San-no-ma (the third room). Jōdan-no-ma is also called Shimyō-no-ma (the Purple Room), and San-no-ma is also called Kujaku-no-ma (the Peacock Room).

KYŌTO CITY CENTER

The center of Kyōto, the area known as Shijō Kawaramachi, is about 15 minutes by bus from Kyōto Station. The district

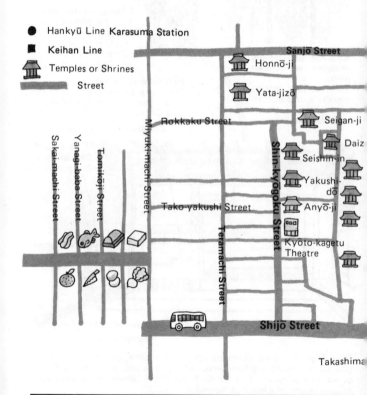

- ● Hankyū Line **Karasuma Station**
- ■ Keihan Line
- 🏛 Temples or Shrines
- ▬ Street

flourished in the Edo Era*, since it was the only place in Kyōto where the authorities would allow *kabuki* to be performed. Many *shibai-goya* (playhouses), *chaya* and *hatago* (inns) were built, and the area became one of the city's largest pleasure districts. It is now a modern shopping area. Gion (see p.60) is located to its east.

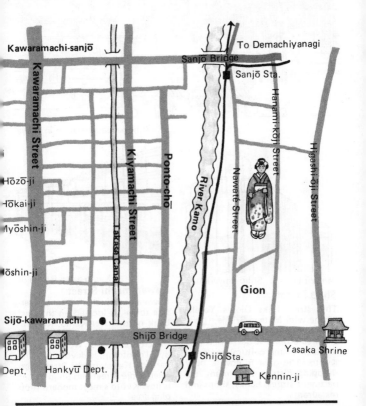

Shijō-kawaramachi in Edo Era

Hankyū Dept. at Shijō-kawaramachi

Kamo-gawa Riverside

Shijō Street

This street links Gion's Yasaka Shrine with Matsuo Bridge. It was constructed in the Heian Era*, and the area around it developed into the artistic and cultural center of Kyōto. The area is now a busy shopping district with many department stores, banks, shops and restaurants.

Kawaramachi Street

Kawaramachi, which means 'riverside town', is located on the west bank of the river Kamo. Kawaramachi Street was built as part of the city renovation works ordered by Toyotomi Hideyoshi*. The part of Kawaramachi Street between Sanjō Street and Shijō Street is now Kyōto's most modern shopping area.

22

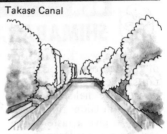

Takase Canal

Ponto-chō

Located between the river Kamo and Kiyamachi Street, Ponto-chō ranks with Gion as one of Kyōto's best-known entertainment districts. At one time, it was also a red-light district. There are many high-class *ryōtei* (Japanese restaurants) and nightclubs here, and it is sometimes possible to glimpse a *maiko** on her way to or from work.

Kiyamachi Street

This street was built in 1611 at the time the Takasé canal was constructed. Kiyamachi means 'timber merchants' town', and it was originally the site of many timber merchants who used the canal to transport logs. Eventually, it became an entertainment district, and the street is now lined with bars.

Shin-kyōgoku

This arcade street is full of shops selling tourist souvenirs. It is fairly new, having been built in 1871. The renovation of the area means that the entrances to a number of temples now lead directly off the street.

Nishiki-kōji

There are about 150 food wholesalers along the 400 m length of this street, and all the ingredients required for cooking in the Kyōto style are sold here. Anybody can wander around and shop here.

●島原

SHIMABARA

Shimabara was Kyōto's first pleasure quarter. At the height of the Genroku period, this area bustled with 24 *ageya* (restaurants where parties attended to be *geisha* dispatched from *okiya* were held). However, with the rise of the pleasure quarters in Gion, this area lost its popularity. All that remains today to give a taste of the original flavor of this area is the east entrance's Daimon (main gate), Wachigai-ya, an *okiya* (an establishment that dispatches *geisha* to *ageya*) and the Sumi-ya (*ageya*).

Kasa (oiled-paper umbrella)

Tortoise-shell combs

Date-hyōgo hair-style

Hana-kanzashi (Ornamental hairpins in the form of flowers)

Kōgai (Hair ornaments)

Uchikaké decorated with gold embroidery

An *uchikaké* is a richly-decorated, long overgarment worn on top of a *kimono*.

Maé-obi style, with the *obi* worn in front.

Hikifuné (attendant)

Tayū

Geta (wooden clogs)

Shimabara Tayū Dōchū

When *tayū* are summoned by customers they put on their best *kimono* and strut grandiosely down the street on their way. This is called *Tayū Dōchū*. This can still be seen every year, on the third Sunday of April, at the Jōshō-ji Temple in Takagamine.

Tayū

Good appearance was not enough to be a *Tayū*. Without training in the traditional Japanese arts: tea ceremony, flower arrangement, *tanka* poetry, dance etc... a *Tayū* could not hope to increase her status.

Shimabara in the Edo Era

During the Edo period, Shimabara flourished as Kyōto's main pleasure quarter. It was known for the *Tayū Dōchū*, barkers who advertised their shop and the many customers who came to browse.

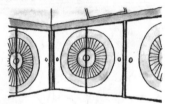

Kasa-no-ma (Umbrella Room)

This is the room where the *kasa* (oiled-paper umbrellas) used by the *tayū* in their procession from *okiya* to *ageya* were kept.

Sumi-ya

Sumi-ya is a typical Shimabara *ageya*. It is a two-storied wooden building in the *Shoin** and *Sukiya* architectural styles, and its gorgeous *fusuma-é* and other furnishings are reminders of the Edo culture.

Wachigai-ya

This is one of Shimabara's typical *okiya*. The symbol of Wachigai-ya is a crest of interlaced circles.

●二条城

NIJŌ CASTLE

This castle was built in 1611 as the Kyōto residence of Toku-gawa Ieyasu*. The *hon-maru* (main court) was burnt down in

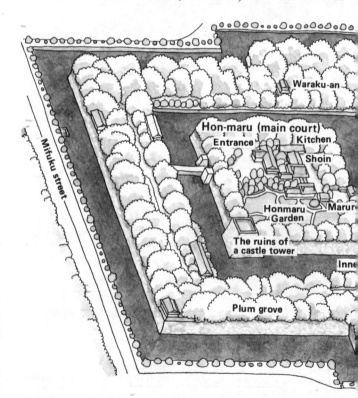

Mifuku street

Waraku-an

Hon-maru (main court)

Entrance

Kitchen

Shoin

Honmaru Garden

Marur

The ruins of a castle tower

Inne

Plum grove

1788, and the only original part remaining is the *ni-no-maru* (second court). The present *hon-maru,* built in 1827, is a copy of the one that originally stood in the grounds of Kyōto Imperial Palace (see p.32). The castle is also famous for its many cultural treasures from the Momoyama Era*, such as the Karamon (Chinese Gate) and Ni-no-maru Garden.

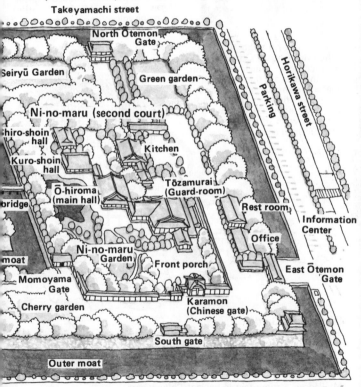

Takeyamachi street

North Ōtemon Gate

Seiryū Garden

Green garden

Horikawa street

Parking

Ni-no-maru (second court)

Shiro-shoin hall

Kuro-shoin hall

Kitchen

Ō-hiroma (main hall)

Tōzamurai (Guard-room)

bridge

Rest room

Information Center

Office

Ni-no-maru Garden

Front porch

moat

East Ōtemon Gate

Momoyama Gate

Cherry garden

Karamon (Chinese gate)

South gate

Outer moat

The *uguisu,* or Japanese bush warbler, is often dubbed nightingale because of its beautiful singing voice.

Uguisubari-no-rōka (the Nightingale Corridor)

This corridor, which leads from the entrance to the *Ō-hiroma,* is specially constructed to give out a noise like the voice of the *uguisu* whenever anyone walks along it, and thus warn of the approach of possible enemies.

Kuruma-yosé (front porch)

The front face of this vestibule is richly carved.

Ni-no-maru Garden

This garden is in the *Tsukiyama** go-round style, with a pond in its center and rocks of various colors and sizes arranged artistically, surrounded by cherry, maple, pine and other trees. The island in the center of the pond represents Mt. Hōrai, a mountain in ancient China where holy men are said to have lived.

Ō-hiroma

The *fusuma-é** in the rooms of the *ni-no-maru* depict mainly *matsu* (pine trees).

The *Matsu-ni-Taka* (pine tree with hawk) in the *Yon-no-ma*.

Gōtenjō
Each room has a different richly-colored pattern on its coffered ceiling.

Ramma
Most of the *ramma* are carved. The one shown here, from the *san-no-ma* features a peacock carved from a 35cm thick piece of *hinoki* (Japanese cypress).

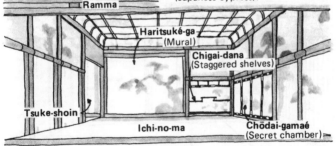

Ramma

Haritsuké-ga (Mural)

Chigai-dana (Staggered shelves)

Tsuke-shoin

Ichi-no-ma

Chōdai-gamaé (Secret chamber)

This large hall, located in the *ni-no-maru*, consists of four rooms and was used by the *shōgun** when holding audiences with his *daimyō**. The *Ichi-no-ma* (first chamber), where the *shōgun* sat in state, is a typical example of the *shoin** style of construction. The *Ni-no-ma* (second chamber) was where the *daimyō* assembled, the *San-no-ma* (third chamber) was their ante-room, and the *Yon-no-ma* (fourth chamber) was where they left their weapons.

NIJŌ JINYA

●二条陣屋

This mansion was originally the home of a wealthy merchant but was also used by the *daimyō** on their visits to Kyōto because of its proximity to Nijō Castle. It contains about 20 rooms, including a tea-ceremony room and a *Noh** hall, and is famous for its various secret contrivances designed to prevent the entry of enemies of the occupants.

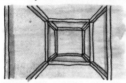

Samurai would lie in wait here

Musha-damari
A trapdoor in the ceiling of the main parlor leads to this small room, which could conceal 4 or 5 *samurai*. Normally, the trapdoor was kept open to admit light via the skylight in the roof.

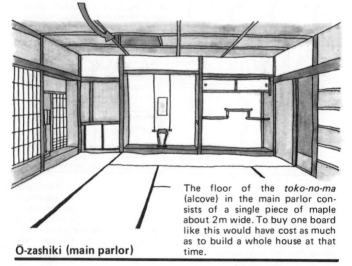

The floor of the *toko-no-ma* (alcove) in the main parlor consists of a single piece of maple about 2m wide. To buy one board like this would have cost as much as to build a whole house at that time.

Ō-zashiki (main parlor)

30　　　　　　　　　　　　　　　*Reservation required

Tsuri-kaidan (trapladder)

The steps to the 2nd floor can be drawn up and appear to form part of the wall. Access to the 2nd floor is through a trapdoor in the ceiling.

To prevent eavesdropping, the partitions between rooms consist of alternate panels of *shōji-gami* (thin, translucent paper) and *fusuma-gami* (thick, opaque paper).This improves the soundproofing and also means that an eavesdropper will cast a shadow on the *shōji* if he approaches too close.

8 of the panels in this wall consist of pairs of boards, while the remaining panels are made of *shōji* paper. The front board of each pair could be lowered to cover the *shōji* panel below it, soundproofing the room.

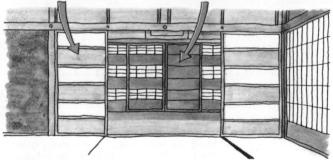

Noh-ma (Noh hall)

The *Noh* hall next to the main parlor was usually used by *samurai** on guard, but could quickly be changed by raising the *tatami** and exposing a stage made of Japanese cypress.

KYŌTO IMPERIAL PALACE

Originally built as the Emperor's second palace, Kyōto Imperial Palace (Kyōto Gosho) was used as the Imperial palace from 1331 to 1867 after the original main palace burnt down. It consists of many large wooden buildings constructed in the *Shinden** style.

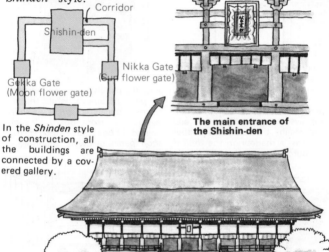

The main entrance of the Shishin-den

In the *Shinden* style of construction, all the buildings are connected by a covered gallery.

Shishinden

This is the main palace of the Kyōto Gosho complex. Also known as Nanden(South Palace), since it occupies the southernmost position, it consists of a single-storey building in the *Irimoya** style. The South Garden is of white sand and is enclosed by three gates and a vermilion-lacquered corridor.

* Reservation required

The Imperial court assembled here from the 17th century on, and a court town under the control of the *shōgun** was built. When the Emperor moved to Tōkyō in 1867, the court town became the present Kyōto Gyoen (Kyōto Imperial Park). This park, which includes the Ōmiya and Sentō Palaces, is also sometimes referred to as Kyōto Gosho.

Ōmiya Palace

This palace, located next to the Sentō Palace, was used by the Emperor's mother. The present building was reconstructed in 1867.

The ruins of Katsura Palace

Ōmiya Palace

Kyōto Palace

Sentō Palace

Hakuun shrine

Munakata shrine

Environment agency

Kyōto Imperial Park

North Pond

Sentō Palace

The Sentō Palace's garden contains two ponds and eight small shrines, and its old trees and rocks convey a mysterious atmosphere of enchantment.

● 京都の正月

NEW YEAR IN KYŌTO

Kyōto boasts a history of over a thousand years, and many of its old ceremonies and customs are still preserved. New Year (*Shōgatsu**) is an ideal time to see some of Kyōto's unique traditional events, both those rooted in the life of the common people and those which recall the elegant and refined culture of the ancient nobility.

Kitchō-nawa

The fire from the lanterns is used to light thin ropes called *kitchō-nawa,* which can then be taken home.

Okera-mairi

On New Year's Eve (*Ōmisoka*) *, a herb called *okera* is burnt in the lanterns at Yasaka Shrine. Those who eat *zōni** cooked over a fire lit from the lanterns are said to be assured of a healthy, happy year.

At New Year, *maiko* put on black *kimono** with a white pattern and wear ears of rice in their hair.

Hatsumōdé

In the custom known as *hatsu-mōdé*, many people visit a shrine on New Year's Day to pray for happiness in the coming year.

Dondo-yaki (Sagichō)

This fire festival is held at *Ko-shō-gatsu*, on Jan. 15. The decorations used at New Year are burnt on a bonfire as a prayer for happiness in the coming year.

初日の出

The higher the sparks from the burning *kaki-zomé* (the first calligraphy of the New Year) fly, the better the writer's calligraphy will become.

Eating *mochi* (rice cakes) toasted on the *Dondo-yaki* fire will keep sickness away for a year.

Karuta-hajimé
This *karuta-kai* (card party), held at Yasaka Shrine on Jan. 3, features the game known as *hyaku-nin-isshu**, in which each card is inscribed with the second half of one of a hundred well-known poems.

Kemari-hajimé
This ball game, introduced from China in the Nara Era*, was a popular pastime among the nobility. This sport is preserved in the *Kemari-hajimé* ceremony practiced at Shimogamo Shrine (see p. 113) on Jan. 4.

KITANO TEMMANGŪ SHRINE

This shrine is dedicated to the Heian Era* scholar Sugawara Michizané, who is revered as a god of learning. After he died of an illness in exile in 903, a series of lightning strikes and outbreaks of fire occurred in Kyōto. People thought these were caused by Michizané wreaking vengeance, and they built Kitano-temmangū Shrine to appease him.

Kaeru-mata
This type of high-relief carving is often seen on beams in traditional Japanese architecture. It is called *kaeru-mata* (frog's legs) because of its appearance.

Sugawara Michizané

Irimoya-style roof

Chidori-hafu

Kara-hafu

The present shrine, rebuilt in 1607, is a typical example of the *Gongen* * architectural style and has a complex roof structure in the *Irimoya* style* with a *Kara-hafu* * and *Chidori-hafu* *. It served as the model for the Tōshōgū Shrine* at Nikkō.

Ema

Ema are small wooden votive tablets carrying a picture of a horse, used as an offering to the shrine in place of a real horse. A wish or prayer is written on the back and the *ema* is then hung up at the shrine.

The Ema-dō (Ema Hall) at Kitano-temmangū Shrine, used specially for this purpose, is the oldest part of the shrine and was built in 1608. Most of the *ema* seen here carry prayers for examination success.

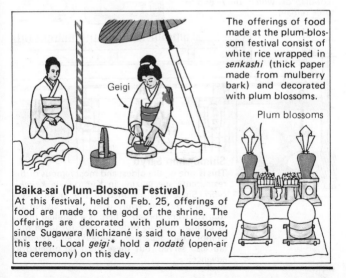

Geigi

The offerings of food made at the plum-blossom festival consist of white rice wrapped in *senkashi* (thick paper made from mulberry bark) and decorated with plum blossoms.

Plum blossoms

Baika-sai (Plum-Blossom Festival)

At this festival, held on Feb. 25, offerings of food are made to the god of the shrine. The offerings are decorated with plum blossoms, since Sugawara Michizané is said to have loved this tree. Local *geigi** hold a *nodaté* (open-air tea ceremony) on this day.

●京料理

KYŌTO-STYLE COOKING

Kyō-ryōri (Kyōto-style cooking) is the name given to the distinctive cooking style that developed from Kyōto's unique geography and customs. It features subtle, rather than strong, flavors, and uses seasonal ingredients to give a sense of the passing of the seasons.

Yūsoku-ryōri

The word *yūsoku* means 'ancient court practice'. This style of cooking started at the court banquets in the Heian Era and established itself as a recognized style in the Muromachi Era*. It subsequently split into various schools, of which only two or three remain.

Shimogamo Saryō

This is one of the oldest and most famous of the restaurants specializing in Kyōto-style *kaiseki-ryōri*. Since it is included in the Japan Travel Bureau's Sunrise Tour, it is often visited by tourists from abroad. There is a detailed menu in English, making ordering easy for those who cannot read Japanese. *Sukiyaki* and *tempura* are also served, but these must be ordered in advance.

Home cooking

Kyōto is a long way from the sea, and the lack of fresh seafood in the Kyōto diet had to be made up for with dried and salted fish and fish taken from the rivers. Another distinctive feature of Kyōto cooking is the extensive use of regional vegetables *(Kyō-yasai)*. Kyōto home cooking is highly varied, and its many unique recipes are still handed down from generation to generation.

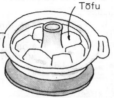

Dried cod   Ebi-imo

Tōfu

Imobō
This well-known Kyōto dish consists of *ebi-imo* (a kind of potato) boiled together with *bōdara* (dried cod).

Yudōfu (boiled tōfu)
Kyōto's *yudōfu* originated in the restaurants near its temples in the latter half of the Edo Era*.

Hamo
The *hamo* (sea eel, or pike conger) has tremendous vitality and can live for a long time out of water, making it an important element in Kyōto cooking.

Shōgoin-kabura
a kind of turnip

Kujō-negi
a variety of leek

Kyō-na
potherb mustard leaf

Kamo-nasu
eggplant

Yuzu
Chinese lemon

Kyō-yasai (Kyōto vegetables)
Since Kyōto is a long way from the sea and the Japanese did not eat meat, vegetables formed a very important part of the Kyōto diet. Many regional vegetables were cultivated, and about thirty of these special Kyōto vegetables are still grown today. They can be bought at the Nishiki-kōji market.

HEIANKYŌ

The area known as *Rakuchū* was divided into 2 parts called *Ukyō*, on the right , and *Sakyō*, on the left, by a street called Suzaku-Ōji.

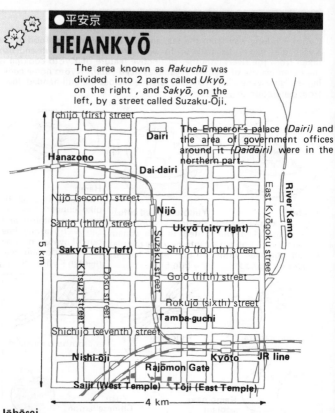

The Emperor's palace *(Dairi)* and the area of government offices around it *(Daidairi)* were in the northern part.

Ichijō (first) street

Dairi

Hanazono

Dai-dairi

Nijō (second) street

Nijō

Sanjō (third) street

Ukyō (city right)

Sakyō (city left)

Shijō (fourth) street

Gojō (fifth) street

Rokujō (sixth) street

Tamba-guchi

Shichijō (seventh) street

Nishi-ōji

Kyōto

JR line

Rajōmon Gate

Saiji (West Temple)   Tōji (East Temple)

Suzaku street

Kitsuzi street

Dōso street

East Kyōgoku street

River Kamo

5 km

4 km

Jōbōsei

Nine Ōji (main streets) starting with Ichijō (First Street) and ending with Kujō (Ninth Street) crossed the city from east to west, while four main streets ran from north to south on either side of the central Suzaku-Ōji. The areas bounded by the main streets were called *bō*, and each of these was subdivided by six narrow streets called *Kōji* into sixteen blocks. The layout of the city was called *jōbōsei*, and it created 1,200 of these small blocks.

40

The emperor Kammu* made Kyōto the capital of Japan in 794. This was the start of the Heian Era*, and the capital was called Heiankyō. The city was modeled on the capital of China in the Tang dynasty. It was located in the area known as Rakuchū, the present center of Kyōto. The only reminder of the original capital left today is the checkerboard layout, called *jōbōsei*, of the part of Kyōto where Heiankyō was located.

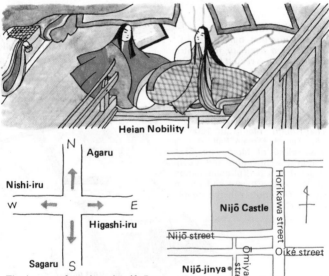

Heian Nobility

The layout of modern-day Kyōto still follows the logical plan of the original capital, and this can be seen in the way addresses are indicated. Any point in the city is indicated by giving the name of the nearest intersection and indicating whether the point is north *("agaru")* or south *("sagaru")* of that intersection.

Nijō Castle is located at Nijōdōri-Horikawa, i.e., at the intersection between Nijō Street and Horikawa Street.

Nijō-jinya is located at Ōmiyadōri-Oiké-Sagaru, i.e., south of the intersection between Ōmiya Street and Oiké Street.

41

●東寺
TŌJI TEMPLE

This temple was built in supplication for national peace at the time Heiankyō was constructed, and was located on the east side of the Rajōmon Gate*, the main gate of the city. The temple on the west side, Saiji Temple, was burnt down in 1233,

Kōdō (Lecture Hall)
This lecture hall, built by Kūkai* in 825 as a seminary for Tantric Buddhism, was rebuilt in the 17th century. Its roof is in the *Irimoya* style.

Kondō (Main Hall)
The Kondō, rebuilt in 1606, is Tōji Temple's main hall. It is a masterpiece of Momoyama-Era* Buddhist architecture, and is constructed in a skillful combination of Japanese, Chinese and Indian styles. The roof is in the double *Irimoya** style.

Nandaimon Gate
This is the main gate of Tōji Temple. The original gate burnt down, and the present one was moved from in front of Sanjūsangen-dō Hall (see p.56) in 1894. Its design is plain, but it boasts eight pillars and a roof in the *Kiritsuma** style.

Taishi-dō hall

Kyakuden hall

Kanchō-in

East gate

Kujō street

42

but Tōji Temple became a seminary for Mikkyō* (Tantric Buddhism) under Kūkai* and eventually developed into the chief Buddhist temple in Japan and the site of all services held to pray for the peace and security of the country.

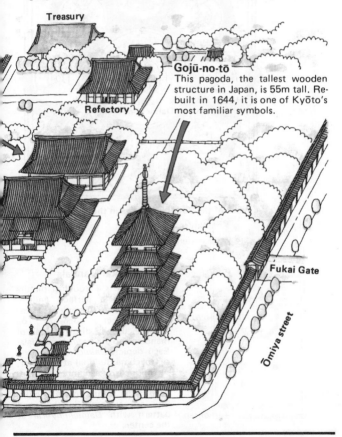

Treasury

Refectory

Gojū-no-tō
This pagoda, the tallest wooden structure in Japan, is 55m tall. Rebuilt in 1644, it is one of Kyōto's most familiar symbols.

Fukai Gate

Ōmiya street

Layout of the Buddhist images in the main hall

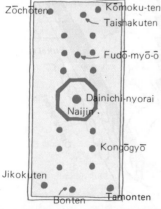

Zōchōten

Kōmoku-ten

Taishakuten

Fudō-myō-ō

Dainichi-nyorai

Naijin

Kongōgyō

Jikokuten

Bonten

Tamonten

The Taizōkai Mandala

A mandala is a Buddhist picture representing a perfect, enlightened universe. Temples of the *Shingon* sect*, such as Tōji Temple, usually display a pair of mandala and a *Kongōkai* mandala. Each depicts *Dainichi-nyorai* (the sun become Buddha) at its center, surrounded by a number of other Buddhas in a circular pattern. The 21 Buddha statues in the Lecture Hall are arranged in the same pattern with *Dainichi-nyorai* at the center.

Sacred pagoda

A sacred spear

Tobatsu Bishamonten

This Buddha, who wields a sacred pagoda in the left hand and a sacred sword in the right, is said to possess the divine power of driving away enemies, and was originally mounted on the Rajō-mon Gate.

Eleven faces

Forty arms

Senju Kannon

Senju Kannon* possesses a thousand arms and a thousand eyes. This statue, created in 877, is the largest wooden statue in Japan.

Circle representing the sun

acred word

Jikokuten

Jikokuten, one of the Four Devas, guards the east. This is one of the finest examples of the *Ichiboku** style of carving.

Fudō-myō-ō

This statue depicts *Dainichi-nyorai* with an angry expression, destroying evil spirits and earthly passions. He is usually depicted sitting on a stone amid a mass of flames. This statue, sculpted in the *Ichiboku* style, is said to be the finest example of its type.

京都の市
KYŌTO FAIRS

The most famous of Kyōto's fairs are *Kōbō-san,* held at Tōji Temple on the 21st of every month, and *Tenjin-san,* held at Kitano-Temmangū Temple on the 25th of every month. Both of these feature open-air stalls selling food, drink, and goods of every description, plus a number selling antiques, sometimes at very reasonable prices.

Comb

Kiyomizu pottery

Kōbō-daishi (Kūkai)

Kōbō-san
Kōbō is another name for Kūkai*, the founder of the Buddhist *Shingon** sect. After he died on 21st Mar., the 21st of every month was designated a fair day. *Hatsu-Kōbō,* on 21st Jan., and *Shimai-Kōbō,* on 21st Dec., are particularly lively.

Glass beads

Antique clock

Pottery

Chawan (teacup)

Glass

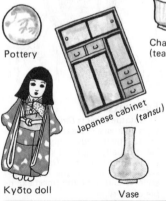

Japanese cabinet (*tansu*)

Tenjin-san
This is the fair day held in memory of Sugawara Michizané* at Kitano-Temmangū shrine. Since he was born on Jun. 25th and died on Feb. 25th, his fair day is held on Jan. 25th and Dec. 25th. Many students visit this fair just before a big examination.

Kyōto doll

Vase

Higashiyama, the east side of
the city, is an area of gentle hills where
many of Kyōto's oldest and
most famous temples and shrines are
concentrated. The walk from Kiyomizu
Temple to Gion is particularly interesting.

HIGASHIYAMA
Kyōto prefecture

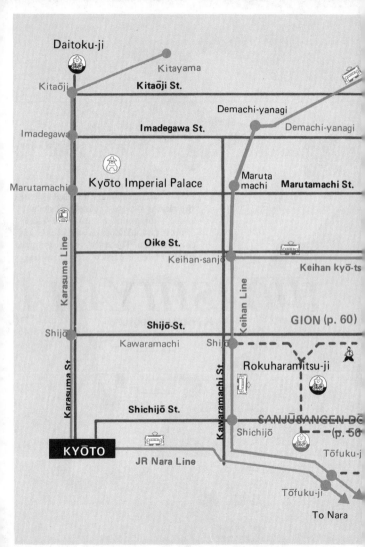

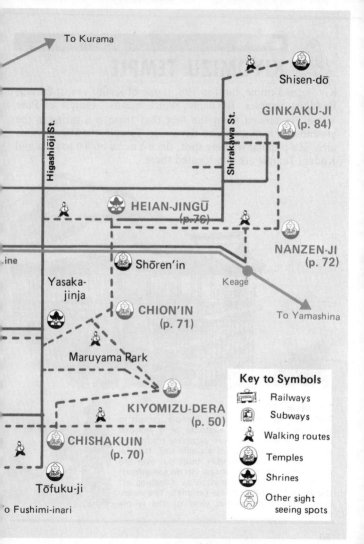

To Kurama

Shisen-dō

GINKAKU-JI
(p. 84)

Higashiōji St.

Shirakawa St.

HEIAN-JINGŪ
(p. 76)

NANZEN-JI
(p. 72)

.ine

Yasaka-
jinja

Shōren'in

Keagé

To Yamashina

CHION'IN
(p. 71)

Maruyama Park

KIYOMIZU-DERA
(p. 50)

CHISHAKUIN
(p. 70)

Tōfuku-ji

o Fushimi-inari

Key to Symbols

	Railways
	Subways
	Walking routes
	Temples
	Shrines
	Other sight seeing spots

KIYOMIZU TEMPLE

Kiyomizu Temple, built in 798, is one of Kyōto's most famous Buddhist temples. Its name, which means "Temple of Pure Water" is derived from the fact that there is a spring in the grounds. The area around Kiyomizu Temple, the Higashiyama area, is a popular walking spot, since Yasaka-no-Tō pagoda and Kōdaiji Temple are also located there.

The Main Hall

The main hall of Kiyomizu Temple, rebuilt in 1633, is an excellent example of a wooden structure built in the pure Japanese traditional style, without the use of a single nail. It is famous for its huge verandah, built out over the cliff, the origin of the phrase (to do something) "with as much determination as if leaping off the verandah at Kiyomizu Temple". The verandah offers a panoramic view of the whole Kyōto.

Saimon (West Gate)

Built in 1607, this eight-pillared gate features elaborate carvings and a roof in the single *Kiritsuma** style. Just inside the gate is the Sanjū-no-Tō (three-storied pagoda).

Otowa-no-Taki (Otowa Falls)

It has been believed since ancient times that the water flowing over this small waterfall in the temple grounds possesses divine power. Drinking the water is said to have beneficial effects such as preventing illnesses.

Umatodomé

When *samurai** came to the temple to pray, they would tether their horses in these stalls at the top of Kiyomizu-zaka, just in front of the Niō-mon Gate. This structure is a valuable relic of the Muromachi Era*.

Koyasu Kannon

This statue of *Koyasu Kannon*, a goddess responsible for the safe delivery of babies, is preserved in the three-storied pagoda south of the main hall. Women have believed in the power of this goddess since ancient times, and even now, many pregnant women visit here.

One of the most popular tourist routes in Kyōto is the road that runs from Kiyomizu Temple via Sannen-zaka and Ninen-zaka to Kōdai-ji Temple and Maruyama Park. This road winds along the foot of Higashiyama (East Mountain), passing many old temples on its way.

Ninen-zaka (Two-year Hill)

This street leading from Sannen-zaka to Kōdaiji, was so named because it is shorter than Sannen-zaka. Most of the houses in this area were built in the Taishō Era*.

Sannen-zaka (Three-year Hill)

The hill known as Sannen-zaka consists of stone steps and links Kiyomizu-zaka with Ninen-zaka. Most of the shops lining the sides of the hill are wooden houses from the Edo Era* (machiya, see p.68), selling Kiyomizu-yaki, antiques, special Kyōto food, and traditional souvenirs of all kinds.

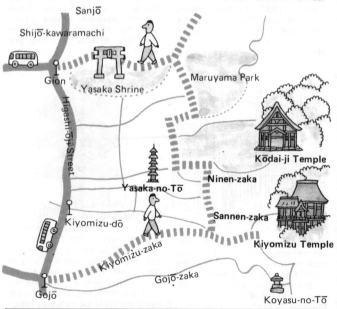

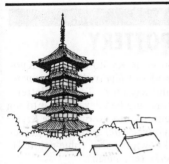

Yasaka-no-Tō

This five-storied pagoda on the west side of Ninen-zaka is the oldest pagoda in Kyōto. Originally part of a temple called Hōkan-ji it was rebuilt in 1440.

The ancestral shrine at Kōdaiji Temple

This shrine, built in 1606 by Kitano Mandokoro* to the memory of her deceased husband Toyotomi Hideyoshi*, houses wooden statues of the couple. It is also famous for its magnificent lacquering, known as *Kōdaiji maki-é*.

The shrine is festooned with *ema* (votive tablets) bearing prayers concerning love.

Jishu Shrine

The god of marriages is enshrined at Jishu Shrine, which is actually within the grounds of Kiyomizu Temple. In front of the main hall is a pair of stones called *Mekura-ishi* ("blind stones") placed 17 to 18 m apart. It is believed that if a person can walk with eyes closed in a straight line from one stone to the other while chanting his or her loved one's name, that love will be fulfilled in marriage.

KIYOMIZU POTTERY

The pottery and ceramics produced in Kyōto are called *Kyō-yaki*. One of the representative styles of *Kyō-yaki* is *Kiyomizu-yaki*, produced in the area around Kiyomizu Temple. Pottery began in Kyōto in the 8th century and had developed into ten different schools by the 17th century, but now only the *Kiyo-mizu-yaki* style is left. Most *Kiyomizu-yaki* consists of porcelain and is divided into types known as *Seiji* (blue-painted), *Aka-é* (red-painted) and *Somé-tsuké* (enameled).

Nonomura Ninsei
This Edo-Era master of painted pottery is said to have had a sense of color and form amounting to genius.

Ogata Kenzan
Together with his elder brother Kōrin, an accomplished painter, this pupil of Ninsei's developed a novel style of painted pottery and created many masterpieces.

Nin'ami Dōhachi
This potter, the most important of the later Edo Era*, is known for his use of a variety of different methods. Besides enameled ware, he also produced pottery in the Chinese and Korean styles.

Kiyomizu Rokubei
Kiyomizu Rokubei, who worked in the Meiji Era*, is particularly famous as a master of the current style of *Kiyomizu-yaki*.

Pottery-Making

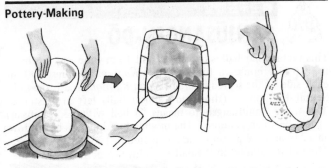

The clay is kneaded with water and shaped on a *rokuro* (potter's wheel).

The pots are fired in a *kama* (kiln).

The fired articles are hand-painted using a *fudé* (brush).

Noborigama

One of the many different types of kiln used in pottery-making in Japan, the *noborigama* consists of a series of rectangular furnaces arranged on a slope. The heat from the bottom furnace rises through the upper furnaces, allowing a large quantity of pottery to be fired in a single firing. All *Kiyomizu-yaki* used to be fired in this type of kiln.

SANJŪSANGEN-DŌ

●三十三間堂

This rectangular hall is 64 m long and 13 m wide and was built in 1164. It houses a total of 1001 *Kannon** statues, 500 on each side of the seated figure of *Senju Kannon*, and is the only Sentai Kannon-dō (thousand-Kannon hall) left in existence. The name Sanjūsangen-dō means "a hall with 33 (sanjūsan) spaces between columns". The original building was burnt down in 1249 and the present one completed in 1266.

Most of the statues in the hall are from this period.

The *Kannon* statues, sculpted in the Kamakura Era*, are arranged in 10 rows of 50 on each side of the center. All the *butsushi* (sculptors of Buddhist carvings) working in Japan at the time are said to have been commissioned to create them. All the statues are covered in gold leaf, filling the dimly-lit hall with a mysterious golden light.

Drumsticks

Drums

Senju Kannon

The seated figure of *Senju Kannon* in the center, flanked by the thousand other sculptures, was created in 1254 by Tankei, one of the most important sculptors of Buddhist images in the Kamakura Era.* This elaborately-carved figure, with its eyes of crystal, is a masterpiece of the *Yoségi** style.

Raijin

Behind the statue of *Senju Kannon* stand the figures of *Fūjin,* the god of wind, and *Raijin,* the god of thunder. *Raijin* carries circular drums on his back and drumsticks in each hand and is depicted gazing down at the earth from Heaven. He makes thunder by beating on the drums.

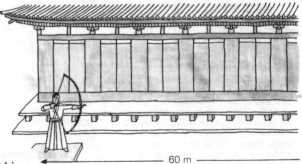

← 60 m →

Tōshi-ya

This *hikizomé* ceremony (the first shooting of an arrow in the New Year) is performed at the west side of the main hall on 15th Jan. The arrows are shot at a 1 m diameter target 60 m (33 *gen)* away, and since the arrows appear to fly through the hall, the ceremony is called *tōshi-ya* (passing arrows). The ceremony was started in the 16th century and was popular among the *samurai** in the Edo Era*.

BUDDHIST STATUES

Buddhism was founded by Sākya-muni in India in the 5th century B.C. and spread through India and China, arriving in Japan in the 6th century A.D. The Buddhism that flourished in Japan was *Daijō-bukkyō* (Mahayana Buddhism), whose followers worship a variety of different Buddhas for different purposes rather than a single Buddha.

The Ichiboku sculpting style

The design of a Yosegi-style sculpture.

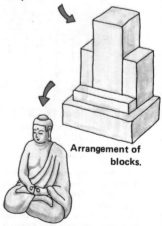

Arrangement of blocks.

The Ichiboku and Yosegi sculpting styles

Although Buddha statues are made of clay, wood, stone, copper, iron and other materials, most of those in Japan are made of wood. In the Nara Era*, Buddha statues were made from a single huge piece of wood, a method of sculpting known as the *Ichiboku* style. However, there was no way of preventing these carvings from splitting when they became old, and so the *Yosegi* method, which uses a number of blocks joined together, became usual.

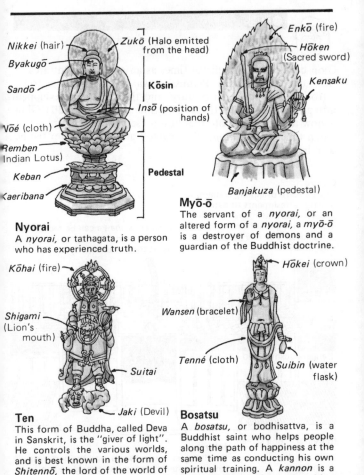

Nyorai

Nikkei (hair)
Byakugō
Sandō
Vōé (cloth)
Remben (Indian Lotus)
Keban
Kaeribana

Zukō (Halo emitted from the head)
Kōsin
Insō (position of hands)
Pedestal

A *nyorai,* or tathagata, is a person who has experienced truth.

Myō-ō

Enkō (fire)
Hōken (Sacred sword)
Kensaku
Banjakuza (pedestal)

The servant of a *nyorai,* or an altered form of a *nyorai,* a *myō-ō* is a destroyer of demons and a guardian of the Buddhist doctrine.

Ten

Kōhai (fire)
Shigami (Lion's mouth)
Suitai
Jaki (Devil)

This form of Buddha, called Deva in Sanskrit, is the "giver of light". He controls the various worlds, and is best known in the form of *Shitennō,* the lord of the world of desire, and *Bonten,* the lord of the physical world.

Bosatsu

Hōkei (crown)
Wansen (bracelet)
Tenné (cloth)
Suibin (water flask)

A *bosatsu,* or bodhisattva, is a Buddhist saint who helps people along the path of happiness at the same time as conducting his own spiritual training. A *kannon* is a female *bosatsu* who ranks with a *nyorai* in the Buddhist hierarchy.

● 祇園

GION

Gion developed in medieval times as an entertainment area in front of Yasaka Shrine. Permission was given for *cha-ya* to be introduced in the 17th century, and the area then developed into a red-light district that rivaled Shimabara (see. p.20). Gion is now the area of Kyōto that best preserves the atmosphere of olden times, and *kimono*-clad *maiko** and *geigi** can often be seen here.

Cha-ya

Cha-ya were originally restaurants serving refreshments to patrons of *kabuki** but later developed into high-class nightclubs where prostitutes known as *cha-ya-onna* plied their trade.

High-class *cha-ya* can be recognized by the *noren* (half-curtain) hung up at the entrance.

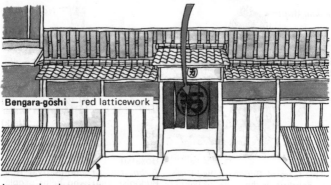

Bengara-gōshi — red latticework

Inu-yarai — dog screen

Ichiriki
Ichiriki was the top *cha-ya,* and the best possible form of entertainment was considered to be to hold a private party here and invite *geigi* to entertain the revelers.

Minami-za

This *kabuki* theater, the oldest in Japan, was built in the 17th century. It is famous for the event known as *Kao-misé*, from the 1st to the 26th of Dec., at which all the actors who will appear the following year are presented on stage. This event is the most important of the year in Gion.

Yasaka Shrine

Located in the northern part of Gion, Yasaka Shrine consists of a *honden* (main hall), *rō-mon* (two-storied gate), *ishi-torii* (stone gate) and other structures, all built in the 17th century. This shrine sponsors the Gion Festival (see p.64).

Ochaya-asobi

Ochaya-asobi is the name given to the form of entertainment in which a dinner party is held at a *cha-ya,* and *maiko* and *geigi* are summoned to entertain the guests. There are 119 *cha-ya* in Gion, but priority is given to regular customers, and it is impossible to visit one of these places without an introduction. The cost is usually about 100,000 yen per guest.

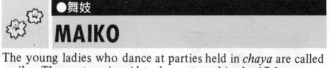

●舞妓

MAIKO

The young ladies who dance at parties held in *chaya* are called *maiko*. The custom is said to have started in the 17th century when the waitresses at *chaya* would imitate *kabuki** for the entertainment of the customers, and at that time, only girls between the ages of 10 and 19 could be *maiko*. Now, the young ladies remain *maiko* until they are about 25, when they graduate to the rank of *geigi*. The tradition of covering their faces with white powder is a sign that they have not yet achieved full status.

Kushi (comb)

Hana-kanzashi

Wareshinobu hairstyle

Dangling *obi*

Long-sleeved *furisodé* kimono

When a *maiko* graduates to the rank of *geigi*, she exchanges her red collar for a white one. This custom is known as *erigaé*.

The *Wareshinobu* hairstyle, the long-sleeved *furisodé* kimono and the dangling *obi* of the *maiko* are reminiscent of the style affected by Edo-era merchants' daughters.

A maiko making up

White face powder is applied all over the face and neck, starting at the bridge of the nose.

Powder is also applied to the back.

Otoko-shi

An assistant known as *otoko-shi* helps the *maiko* put on her *kimono*.

The hair is correctly adjusted.

Bright-red lipstick is used.

Wareshinobu hairstyle   *Ofuku* hairstyle

Two typical hairstyles

There are strict rules for the type of hairstyle, depending on the situation.

Hana-kanzashi (an ornamental hairpin in the form of flowers)

Mai-ōgi (a folding fan used when dancing)

A maiko's accessories

●祇園まつり
GION MATSURI

The Gion Festival is a huge festival that starts on Jul. 1st and continues for a month. It was said to have been started in 869 in the hope of securing divine intervention to halt an epidemic that was raging at the time. The festival took its current form in the Edo Era*, when the gorgeously-decorated festival floats known as *yama* and *hoko* first made their appearance. The main events of the festival are *Yoi-yama*, on the 16th, and *Yamahoko-junkō*, on the 17th.

The *hoko* each carry a *hayashi**
(festival music) orchestra of about
40 members.

Yamahoko-junkō

The 23 *yama* appearing in this parade are 6 m tall and weigh 1.5 tons, while the 8 *hoko* are 25 m tall and weigh 12 tons. Most of them were made in the 15th century, and they are embellished with luxurious tapestries and decorations imported from Belgium, Persia, Turkey and other countries. This parade is the highlight of the Gion Festival.

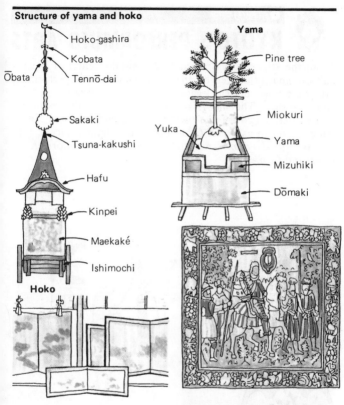

Structure of yama and hoko

Hoko-gashira
Kobata
Tennō-dai
Ōbata
Sakaki
Tsuna-kakushi
Hafu
Kinpei
Maekaké
Ishimochi
Hoko

Yama
Pine tree
Miokuri
Yuka
Yama
Mizuhiki
Dōmaki

Byōbu Matsuri

At *Yoi-yama,* people open the doors of their houses in the custom known as *Byōbu Matsuri* (the Screen Festival) to show those attending the festival their treasured old folding screens.

Rear view of Niwatori-hoko

The Belgian tapestry used to decorate the rear of the *Niwatori-hoko* depicts ancient Roman legends. This tapestry, woven in the 14th and 15th centuries, offers evidence that Kyōto was a thriving trade center at the time.

KYŌTO'S PERFORMING ARTS

From the 8th century onward, Kyōto was the center of Japan's culture, and influenced by the aristocracy, various performing arts were born, either elegant and refined or dazzling in their showmanship. The most famous of these are the exquisite dances performed by the *maiko** and *geigi** of Gion. These dances, known as *Godai Odori* (The Five Major Dances), consist of *Miyako-odori, Kamogawa-odori, Kitano-odori, Kyō-odori* and *Gion-odori.*

Miyako-odori
paper lantern

Miyako-odori (the Cherry Dance)

This original and entertaining performance has become one of the biggest attractions of Kyōto in spring. The dancers perform together in a group against a backdrop of cherry blossoms, with cries of *"Yoi-yasaa!"*. The performance can be seen at Gion Kōbu-kaburenjō from the 1st to the 30th of Apr.

Kitano-odori
Compared with the gay and extravagant dances that originated in the pleasure quarters of old Japan, this dance is more restrained and theatrical. It is performed at Kitano Kaikan Hall from the 15th to the 25th of Apr.

Kamogawa-odori
This dance is performed at Ponto-chō Kaburenjō by the *geigi* of Ponto-chō (see p. 23) from the 1st to the 24th of May and from Oct. 15th to Nov. 7th.

ryūgasa

Hanagasa (flower hat) decorated with plum blossoms.

Hanezu-odori
In this performance, young girls wearing *hanezu-iro* (pale pink) *kimono* enact the legend of Ono-no Komachi*, dancing round *fū-ryūgasa** placed on a stage set among plum trees. It can be seen at Zuishin-in Temple on Mar. 30th.

Shamenchi-odori
Young girls wearing *hanagasa* (flower hats) dance round young boys in girls' *kimono* with *tōrō** (lanterns) on their heads. This dance is performed at Yase Tenman-gū Shrine on 10th Oct.

KYŌTO HOUSES

The houses of Kyōto merchants are called *machi-ya*, and their sensible layouts and aesthetic appeal make them the best of Japan's city dwellings. Most *machi-ya* are low, two-storey buildings, known colloquially as *"unagi-no-nedoko"* ('eels' beds') because of the way the rooms are laid out end-to-end.

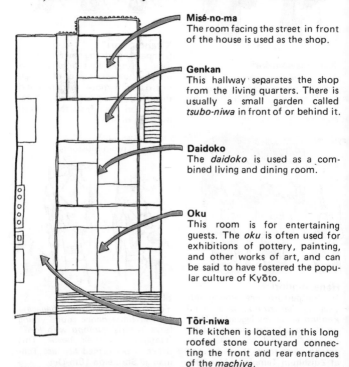

Misé-no-ma
The room facing the street in front of the house is used as the shop.

Genkan
This hallway separates the shop from the living quarters. There is usually a small garden called *tsubo-niwa* in front of or behind it.

Daidoko
The *daidoko* is used as a combined living and dining room.

Oku
This room is for entertaining guests. The *oku* is often used for exhibitions of pottery, painting, and other works of art, and can be said to have fostered the popular culture of Kyōto.

Tōri-niwa
The kitchen is located in this long roofed stone courtyard connecting the front and rear entrances of the *machiya*.

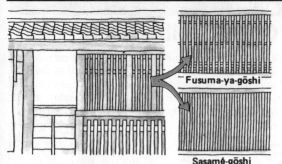

Fusuma-ya-gōshi

Sasamé-gōshi

A mushiko window in the front hall

This type of window consists of closely-spaced, narrow slats, enabling those inside to see out while preventing passers-by from looking in.

The *kōshi*, or latticework, on Kyōto's *machi-ya* is made from thin slats and is also known as *senbon-gōshi* (thousand-slat lattice). There are various designs depending on the type of shop.

Stone lantern

Tsukubai

Hakodan

The history of *machiya* has also been a history of the struggle with lack of space. Stairs in the form of chests of drawers are one example of this struggle.

Tsubo-niwa

This small garden is located between the shop and the living quarters. Kyōto merchants would put all their financial resources into this garden, making it a symbol of opulence and spaciousness amid their cramped surroundings.

●智積院

CHISHAKU-IN TEMPLE

This temple, built by Toyotomi Hideyoshi* to the memory of his eldest son, is famous for the twenty-five murals in the *Dai-shoin hall* and for its beautiful *Tsukiyama*-style* garden. The art treasures of the temple are put on public display at the *Aoba Matsuri* festival held every year on Jun. 15, the birthday of Kōbō-daishi*.

Sakura-no-ma (the Cherry Room) in the Dai-shoin hall

Sakura-zu

Although this picture of a cherry tree resembles that of the maple, the graceful branches and the beautiful coloring of the blossoms give it a nobility and refinement exceeding mere magnificence.

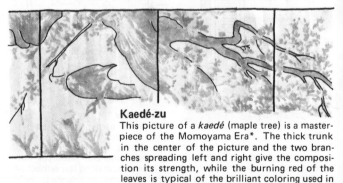

Kaedé-zu

This picture of a *kaedé* (maple tree) is a masterpiece of the Momoyama Era*. The thick trunk in the center of the picture and the two branches spreading left and right give the composition its strength, while the burning red of the leaves is typical of the brilliant coloring used in pictures of this period.

70

●知恩院
CHION-IN TEMPLE

The headquarters of the *Jōdo-shū** sect, Chion-in was established in 1211 when Hōnen* founded a Zen* school here. It was expanded in the Edo Era* with the assistance of the Tokugawa* family and was transformed into a huge temple with 17 halls and 5 gates. It is also the repository of the legends known as the Seven Mysteries.

Uryū-seki
An *uri* (melon) with the name of the god Gozu Tennō inscribed on it is said to have grown out of this rock one night.

Sampō-mamuki no Neko
No matter from what direction it is viewed, the cat in this picture always appears to be facing straight at the viewer.

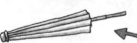

A *kasa* (oiled-paper umbrella) was left under the roof at the front. It is said to have been left there by the carpenters who built the hall, as a charm to ward off evil.

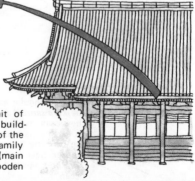

Main Hall
Built to house the portrait of *Hōnen* in 1639, this wooden building was one of the symbols of the power of the Tokugawa family along with the *Sammon* (main gate), one of the largest wooden gates in Japan.

●南禅寺
NANZEN-JI TEMPLE

As the main temple of the *Rinzai-shū** Nanzen-ji sect, this temple was built in 1291. Its grounds were expanded to more than 300,000 m² in the Edo Era*. From the *Sammon* (main gate), *Hōjō* (head priest's residence) and gardens to the paintings and other objects that decorate the rooms, everything to be found in this temple is a beautiful example of 13th – 17th century Japanese art and craft.

Tora-no-ko-watashi

Shangri-la

Ocean

Hōjō Garden
This rectangular garden is a typical example of the *karé-sansui**-style. Its white sand represents the ocean, while its rocks and plants represent an earthly paradise, or Shangri-la, lying far over the sea. The 2 rocks separated by sand depict a mother tiger with her cub, and are known as *Tora-no-ko-watashi* ("tiger cub crossing the ocean").

Sammon

A panoramic view of Kyōto can be had from the top of this huge wooden gate, built in 1627. The legendary robber Ishikawa Goemon* was said to have exclaimed the words *"Zekkei kana!"* ("What a fantastic view!") when he first stood here.

Ishikawa Goemon

The famous robber Ishikawa Goemon became enshrined in legend as Japan's greatest robber after being made the hero of the Edo-Era* *kabuki* play. The *sammon* (main gate) of Nanzen-ji Temple appears in this play in the scene *"Sammon Gosan-no-Kiri"*.

Mizunomi-no-Tora

The *Tora-no-ma* (Tiger Room) in the *Shōjō* Hall features 39 murals depicting tigers. The most famous of these, a masterpiece of the *Kanō* school, is the *Mizunomi-no-Tora* ("Drinking Tiger").

Yudōfu

Many of the restaurants around Nanzen-ji specialize in the famous Kyōto dish *yudōfu* (boiled *tōfu*). This dish tastes best in the cherry-blossom season or fall, when the grounds of this temple are at their most beautiful.

SHŌJIN-RYŌRI

The word *shōjin*, written with the characters for "spirit" and "advance", means forswearing evil and following the path of righteousness, i.e., following the Buddhist way. The food eaten by Buddhist priests of the *Zenshū** sect thus came to be known as *Shōjin-ryōri*, or "*Shōjin* cooking". This style of cooking, which originally came from China, is a form of vegetarian cooking, since it uses neither fish nor meat.

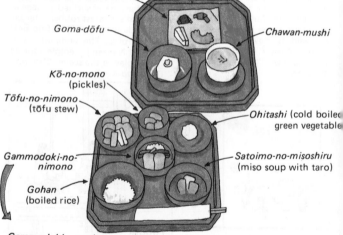

Hassun (vinegared dish)

Goma-dōfu

Chawan-mushi

Kō-no-mono (pickles)

Tōfu-no-nimono (tōfu stew)

Ohitashi (cold boiled green vegetable)

Gammodoki-no-nimono

Satoimo-no-misoshiru (miso soup with taro)

Gohan (boiled rice)

Gammodoki, made by frying tōfu with yama-imo (yam) and other vegetables, was popular among priests in the days when eating meat was forbidden.

Shōjin-ryōri is divided into two main types, *Gyōhatsu-ryōri* and *Fucha-ryōri*. In the former type, eating is considered to be part of Buddhist training and is regulated by strict rules, while in the latter type, it is treated as a more pleasurable occupation.

Chawan-mushi
This dish normally consists of steamed egg custard with vegetables, but, in *Shōjin ryōri*, *yamato-imo* (a type of yam) is substituted for the egg.

Yasai-no-Nimono
One of the main dishes in *Shōjin-ryōri* is vegetables stewed in a broth flavored with soy sauce. Various vegetables are used, including *daikon* (Japanese radish) and *renkon* (lotus root).

Kōya-dōfu
An indispensable ingredient of *Shōjin-ryōri*, *kōya-dōfu* consists of *tōfu* frozen and then dried.

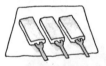

Dengaku-dōfu
This dish consists of small rectangles of *tōfu* placed on a skewer, toasted over a fire, and eaten with flavored *miso**.

Shōjin-agé
Shōjin-agé is *tempura** made with vegetables only.

Goma-dōfu
This food does not actually contain any *tōfu*, it only resembles it. It consists of *kuzuko* (kudzu starch) flavored with *shiro-goma* (white sesame) and smoked.

Namafu-no-agemono
This dish consists of fried *namafu* (raw wheat gluten), a food often used in Kyōto cooking.

Miso-shiru
The *miso-shiru* (miso soup) contains vegetables of the season.

Hassun
Originally the name of the small lacquered tray on which the food is served, "hassun" now refers to the food itself.

●平安神宮
HEIAN SHRINE

This is one of Kyōto's newer shrines, having been built in 1895 to mark the eleven hundredth anniversary of the construction of *Heiankyō* (see p.40). It is a reconstruction to 5/8 scale of buildings that stood in the Imperial Court of the Heian Era*, and it gives us the flavor of that era even though the old capital no longer exists.

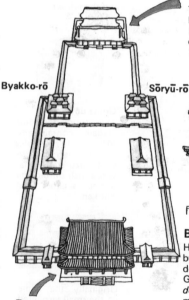

Byakko-rō

Sōryū-rō

Daigoku-den Hall
The main government hall in the Heian Era*, this was where the Emperor would conduct the affairs of state. It was burnt down in 1177 and has never been rebuilt.

Byakko-rō
Heian Shrine consists of eight buildings linked by a long corridor running from the *Ōten-mon* Gate in the north to the *Daigoku-den* hall in the south. Two of the most interesting structures are the *Byakko-rō* (White tiger) and *Sō-ryū-rō* (Blue Dragon) towers, renowned for their intricate construction.

Ōten-mon Gate
This garden-roofed, two-storied gate is a replica of the main gate of the *Heian-kyō* Imperial Court.

The Emperor Kammu (737 - 806)
Heian Shrine is dedicated to two emperors, Kammu and Kōmei. Kyōto's thousand-year history started when the Emperor Kammu moved the capital of Japan, *Heijō-kyō**, from its site at Nara to Kyōto, renaming it *Heian-kyō*.

The Emperor Kōmei(1831—1866)
The Emperor Kōmei was the last emperor to have his palace at Kyōto. The emperor who succeeded him, the Emperor Meiji, moved to Tōkyō, bringing to an end Kyōto's history as an Imperial city.

Kagura-den Hall
Imperial ceremonies were held in this hall, which is now used for weddings.

At a Japanese-style wedding, the bride and groom make their wedding vows before a *kannushi,* or *Shintō* priest. This style of ceremony is called *shinzen-kekkon* ("wedding before the gods").

Some everyday objects used by the emperor

Ivory incense holder and
incense burner

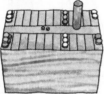

Sugoroku *
(dice game) board

Kai-awasé
A diversion practiced by the nobility of the *Heian* Era, *Kai-awasé*
was a game in which 360 clam
shells were split into two halves,
shuffled, and divided equally between two players. The player
who had the most matching
halves in his pile was the winner.

Takigi-noh
This form of *noh* * is so called because it is performed at night in the
open air, and lighting is provided by burning firewood *(takigi)*. The
best-known performances are those given at Nara's Kōfuku-ji Temple.
In Kyōto, it is performed on 1st and 2nd Jun. on a special stage constructed in front of Heian Shrine's Daigokuden Hall.

Okazaki Park

This huge park, adjacent to Heian Shrine, has an area of 103,101 m² and contains a zoo, exhibition halls and art museums, a sports ground, and a library. It is a popular place on holidays.

A Biwako Sosui — this 11.1 km canal runs from Lake Biwa, Japan's largest lake, to the center of Kyōto. It was built in 1890 for electric power generation and ship transport.

B Kyōto Assembly Hall — used for international conferences and cultural events

C Kyōto Exposition Hall — used for exhibitions of Kyōto's modern industry.

D Kyōto Hall of Traditional Industry — used for exhibitions of Kyōto's traditional industry. A replica of a *machi-ya* (see p. 68) is on display here.

E Kyōto Museum of Art — houses a collection consisting mainly of modern Japanese art

F Kyōto National Museum of Modern Art — famous for its large collection of ceramics and woodblock prints.

●時代まつり
JIDAI MATSURI

One of Kyōto's three biggest festivals along with the *Gion* Festival (see p.64) and the *Aoi* Festival (see p.114), the *Jidai Matsuri* consists of a huge costumed parade depicting Japan's history and culture in 17 groups from the Meiji Era* back through the ages to the Heian Era*, and has been held every year since 1885. The festival takes place on Oct. 22.

Ishin Kinnō-tai procession
(Meiji Era)
This procession depicts the *kangun* (Imperial army) at the time of the *Meiji* Restoration*.

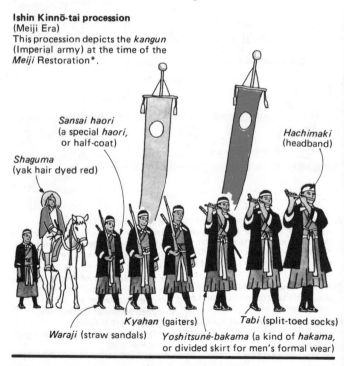

Sansai haori (a special *haori*, or half-coat)

Hachimaki (headband)

Shaguma (yak hair dyed red)

Kyahan (gaiters)

Waraji (straw sandals)

Yoshitsuné-bakama (a kind of *hakama*, or divided skirt for men's formal wear)

Tabi (split-toed socks)

80

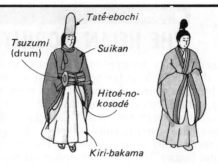

Taté-ebochi

Tsuzumi
(drum)

Suikan

Hitoé-no-
kosodé

Kinugasa
(silk cape)

Kiri-bakama

Edo-Era* ladies
The Lady Kazu-no-Miya* is seen here at the age of 16, as yet unmarried, wearing the formal dress of an *Edo*-Era court lady.

Medieval court ladies
Shizuka Gozen was the mistress of Mina-moto-no-Yoshitsuné*. She is wearing *shira-byōshi,* a dancer's costume of the Kamakura Era*.

Heian-Era ladies
This poetess of the early Heian Era, Ono-no-Komachi, was said to have been an unsurpassed beauty.

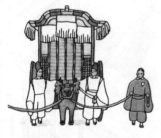

Hōkō Sanchō procession
(Azuchi-Momoyama Era)
This part of the parade depicts *Hōkō* (Toyotomi Hideyoshi*) and his retinue proceeding to pay their respects to the Emperor. It features an elaborately-decorated *gissha* (ox-drawn carriage).

Warriors of the Enryaku Era*
This procession of 9th-century warriors shows the earliest uniforms worn by Japanese *samurai*.

81

THE HEIAN NOBILITY

Japanese society became stratified into various social classes with the Emperor at the top in about the 5th century A.D. The top government was formed from members of the aristocracy, which continued to monopolize the political power through the Nara* and Heian* Eras, increasing in pomp and splendor. However, it failed either to manage its agricultural fiefs successfully or to suppress the rise of the *buké*, the great *samurai* houses. This led to the gradual waning of the nobility's power, and from the Kamakura Era* on, its role dwindled to that of a preserver of culture and tradition. The noble houses are also known as *kugé*.

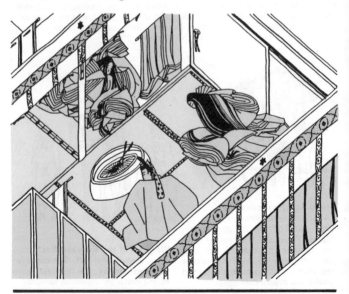

Make-up

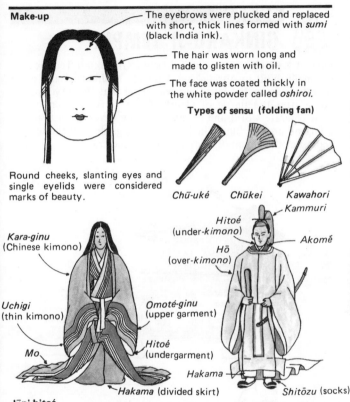

The eyebrows were plucked and replaced with short, thick lines formed with *sumi* (black India ink).

The hair was worn long and made to glisten with oil.

The face was coated thickly in the white powder called *oshiroi*.

Round cheeks, slanting eyes and single eyelids were considered marks of beauty.

Types of sensu (folding fan)

Chū-uké   *Chūkei*   *Kawahori*

Kammuri

Kara-ginu (Chinese kimono)

Uchigi (thin kimono)

Mo

Omoté-ginu (upper garment)

Hitoé (undergarment)

Hakama (divided skirt)

Hitoé (under-*kimono*)

Hō (over-*kimono*)

Akomé

Hakama

Shitōzu (socks)

Jūni-hitoé
Formal wear for ladies, the *jūni-hitoé* consisted of a *kimono* called *hitoé* on top of which were worn up to 20 or more thin *kimono* called *uchigi*. An elegant effect was achieved by choosing the best combination of different-colored collars and sleeves.

Sokutai
The *sokutai*, full court dress for men, consisted of *hakama* (a kind of divided skirt) and a five-layerd *kimono*. Civilian and military officials wore different types of *sokutai,* and ranks were distinguished by the color of the *kimono*.

83

GINKAKU-JI TEMPLE

One of Kyōto's most beautiful sights, Ginkaku-ji Temple was originally built by the *shōgun* Ashikaga Yoshimasa* as a place of refuge from the burnt-out wasteland that the city had become after the Battle of Ōnin*. There he tried to create his own separate world and escape from the devastation that was going on around him. The buildings and gardens of the temple represent the cream of *Muromachi** art and craft.

The second story is in the Chinese Buddhist-hall style.

The first storey is constructed in the Japanese *Shinden** style

Ginkaku (the Silver Pavilion)
This two-storied building is a *Kannon** hall with a double roof in the *Hōgyō** style. The first storey was used as a residence, while the second was a *Butsuma* (Buddhist altar room) housing a statue of *Kannon**. *Ginkaku-ji* is so called to distinguish it from *Kinkaku-ji* (Golden Pavilion, see p. 100) and is not actually silvered.

Ginkaku-ji Garden

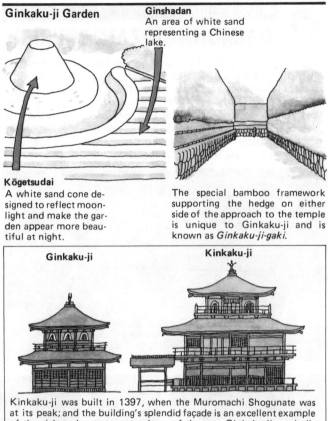

Ginshadan
An area of white sand representing a Chinese lake.

Kōgetsudai
A white sand cone designed to reflect moonlight and make the garden appear more beautiful at night.

The special bamboo framework supporting the hedge on either side of the approach to the temple is unique to Ginkaku-ji and is known as *Ginkaku-ji-gaki*.

Ginkaku-ji

Kinkaku-ji

Kinkaku-ji was built in 1397, when the Muromachi Shogunate was at its peak; and the building's splendid façade is an excellent example of the rich and extravagant culture of the age. Ginkaku-ji was built 92 years later, in 1489, when civil war had turned Kyōto into a burnt-out wasteland and the people, despairing for the future, had turned to religion in the hope of achieving happiness in the after-life. The mood of these times is reflected in the awesome beauty of this building, a beauty somehow tinged with sadness.

●大文字五山送り火
DAIMONJI GOZAN OKURIBI

Held on Aug. 16, this festival is one of the rites of *bon**, in which fires called *okuribi* are lit to speed the souls of people's ancestors back on their way after their yearly visit to this world. In the *Daimonji* festival, fires are lit on five hills (*Gozan*) around Kyōto, in the shape of the Chinese characters *dai* ("large"), *myō* ("miraculous") and *hō* ("doctrine"), and in the form of a ship *(Funagata)* and a *torii**. Various other *bon* ceremonies are held in Kyōto at this time.

The fires representing the character *dai* are lit on Mt. Nyoigataké at 8:00 p.m.

Large numbers of fire engines stand by in case of forest fires.

Myō (at left) and *Hō* (at right). Lit on Mt. Mantōrō and on Mt. Daikokuten at 8:10 p.m.

Funagata (ship). Mt. Myōkenzan, 8:15 p.m.

Torii-gata (torii). Mt. Mandala 8:20 p.m.

Firewood
Pine needles
Chimney
Ōya-ishi stones

Sectional view of fire grates
Pine logs are stacked criss-cross fashion on a stone hearth, and the resulting structure is filled with pine branches with the needles attached.

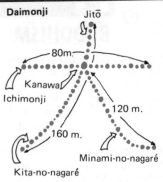

Daimonji
Jitō
80m.
Kanawa
Ichimonji
120 m.
160 m.
Minami-no-nagaré
Kita-no-nagaré

Mantō-é
Lanterns are lit at the beginning of *bon* as *mukaebi**, fires lit to welcome the souls of ancestors back to this world. This custom is known as *Mantō-é*. At the end of *bon*, the lanterns are floated down the rivers to the sea as *okuribi**, in the ceremony known as *Mantō-nagashi*.

Rokudō-mairi
The legendary road linking this world with the spirit world is called *Rokudō*. It is believed that if one stands on this road beating a gong and calling out one's ancestors' names, the sound will guide the dead souls back to this world. *Rokudō* is said to lie in the vicinity of Chinkō-ji Temple, which is near a large graveyard.

●仏教

BUDDHISM

Buddhism *(bukkyō)* was introduced to Japan from Korea in the 6th century and was adopted as the state religion. The end of the Heian Era*, however, was an age of war and unrest, and the *fin-de-siècle* mood led to the birth of the individualistic Zen sect and the escapist *Jōdo* sect. All of Japan's important Buddhist sects were formed by this time. Buddhism was replaced by *Shintō* as the state religion in the Meiji Era, and the *Haibutsu-Kishaku* movement attempted to eradicate the former religion. However, it survived, and, since that time, Buddhism and *Shintō* have enjoyed equal popularity, with most of Japan's population following both religions simultaneously.

The Shingon-shū sect
(Heian Era)
This sect, founded by *Kūkai*, teaches the mystic doctrine that by chanting *shingon* (words of truth) and entering into a spirit of Buddhahood, it is possible to become a living Buddha.

The Tendai-shū sect
(Heian Era)
This sect bases its teachings on a holy scripture called *Hokekyō*, said to be the most mystical of all the Buddhist doctrines. The sect was introduced into Japan by the priest *Saichō* and was the precursor of the *Zen, jōdo* and *Nichiren* sects.

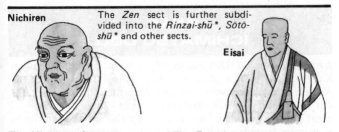

Nichiren

The *Zen* sect is further subdivided into the *Rinzai-shū**, *Sōtō-shū** and other sects.

Eisai

The Nichiren-shū sect
(Kamakura Era)

This sect was founded by the priest *Nichiren* in the 13th century. It teaches that the *Hokekyō* is the single and absolute source of truth, and that any person is capable of achieving oneness with the Buddha simply by reciting its words.

The Zen-shū sect (Kamakura Era)

Zen is a form of Buddhist training in which the acolytes bring themselves through meditation to the point where they are capable of receiving instant enlightenment. The *Zen* sect regards this as the most important form of training and places more emphasis on individual enlightenment than on the salvation of the people as a whole.

Hōnen

The Jōdo-shū sect
(Kamakura Era)

This sect, founded by *Hōnen,* is also known as the Pure Land sect. It teaches that anyone can save themselves by believing in *Amida** (Amitabha) and chanting the phrase *namu-amida-butsu.* The simplicity of this doctrine led to its swiftly becoming popular, but the authorities suppressed it because of its escapist tendencies, and it eventually went into decline.

Shinran

The Jōdo-Shinshū sect
(Kamakura Era)

The priest Shinran developed this sect, an offshoot of the *Jōdo* sect. It is famous for the huge army of *sōhei* (fighting monks) that it formed in the Sengoku Era*. Since it taught the doctrine of reincarnation, the monks were said to have absolutely no fear of death.

市松人形
ICHIMATSU DOLLS

Ichimatsu Ningyō (Ichimatsu dolls) were first produced in Kyōto in the middle of the Edo Era* as representations of the *Kabuki* actor Sanogawa Ichimatsu. With their black, classically-cut hair, chubby cheeks and single eyelids, these dolls enjoyed great popularity. Their mysterious expression has given rise to numerous legends, such as that they occasionally fall in love with their maker, where upon their hair starts to grow of its own accord.

Creating an Ichimatsu doll

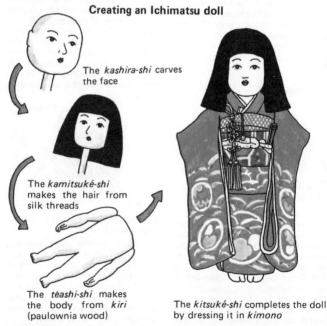

The *kashira-shi* carves the face

The *kamitsuké-shi* makes the hair from silk threads

The *téashi-shi* makes the body from *kiri* (paulownia wood)

The *kitsuké-shi* completes the doll by dressing it in *kimono*

The steep mountains of Rakuhoku, the north side of the city, thought since ancient times to be the haunt of devils and evil spirits, were used by priests and monks for their ascetic practices. Even though the area is now crossed by a modern road network, its mysterious atmosphere remains.

RAKUHOKU

Kyōto prefecture

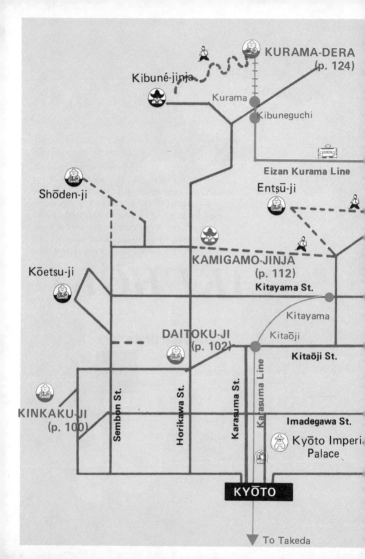

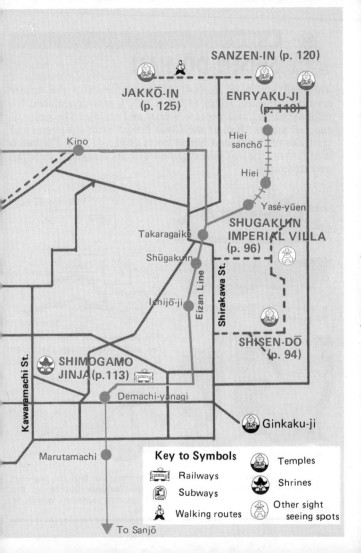

SANZEN-IN (p. 120)

JAKKŌ-IN
(p. 125)

ENRYAKU-JI
(p. 118)

Kino

Hiei
sanchō

Hiei

Yasé-yūen

Takaragaike

SHUGAKUIN
IMPERIAL VILLA
(p. 96)

Shūgakuin

Eizan Line

Shirakawa St.

Ichijō-ji

SHISEN-DŌ
(p. 94)

Kawaramachi St.

SHIMOGAMO
JINJA (p.113)

Demachi-yanagi

Ginkaku-ji

Marutamachi

To Sanjō

Key to Symbols

🚋 Railways

🚇 Subways

🚶 Walking routes

🛕 Temples

⛩ Shrines

🏯 Other sight
seeing spots

SHISEN-DŌ HALL

This hall was built in 1641 as the residence of the former *samurai* Ishikawa Jōzan (1583 – 1672), who abandoned his military calling and became a poet and recluse. The name of the hall means "Hall of the Great Poets" after the poems and portraits of thirty six Chinese poets displayed in it. The hall is also famous for its Chinese garden with its man-made waterfall and streams.

A view of the Shōgetsu-rō from the garden.

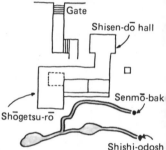

The stream flows from the waterfall and runs through the center of the garden to the *shishi-odoshi*.

Senmō-baku

This artificial waterfall to the south-east of the hall is the source of the stream that flows through the garden.

The white sand and the rounded *tsutsuji* (azalea) bushes in the front garden represent islands in the sea.

Fig. 1　　　　　Fig. 2　　　　　Fig. 3

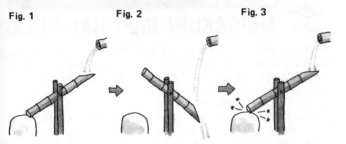

Shishi-odoshi

When the bamboo pipe fills with water (Fig. 1), it swings down and releases the water (Fig. 2). It then swings back to its original position and strikes a stone, emitting a hollow "tonk", and starts to fill with water again (Fig. 3).

The name *shishi-odoshi* means "animal-scarer", but this device is often used in classical Japanese gardens because of the serene quality of the sound it makes. It is also called *sōzu*.

The hall contains portraits of famous Chinese poets and copies of their poems.

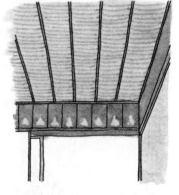

The *Shisen-no-Ma* (Poets' Room) features an *ampera* (rush) ceiling and a carving representing a fan.

● 修学院離宮

SHUGAKUIN IMPERIAL VILLA

Together with Katsura Imperial Villa (see p.148), Shugakuin Imperial Villa, built in 1659, is one of the most important mountain villas of the early Edo Era*. The extensive go-round-style gardens consist of an upper garden *(Kami-no-Chaya)* and a lower garden *(Shimo-no-Chaya),* completed in 1659, and a middle garden *(Naka-no-Chaya)* completed in 1682. The villa, tea-ceremony houses, a temple and other buildings are dotted about the gardens. The view from the Rin'un-tei pavilion in the upper garden is particularly famous.

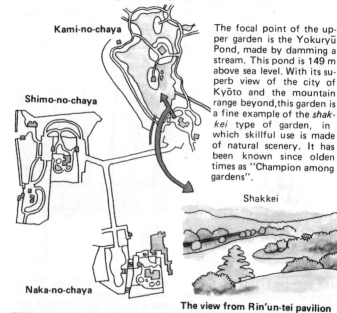

Kami-no-chaya

Shimo-no-chaya

Naka-no-chaya

The focal point of the upper garden is the Yokuryū Pond, made by damming a stream. This pond is 149 m above sea level. With its superb view of the city of Kyōto and the mountain range beyond, this garden is a fine example of the *shakkei* type of garden, in which skillful use is made of natural scenery. It has been known since olden times as "Champion among gardens".

Shakkei

The view from Rin'un-tei pavilion

*Reservation required

The Bōfū-tei summerhouse and the small three-tiered stone pagoda of Rinkyū-ji temple are behind the Kyakuden hall. This pagoda also called *Higaki-no-Tō,* is said to have been imported from Korea.

Rakushi-ken

This house was built in the middle garden as a residence for the Emperor's sister. It is simply-constructed but employs a novel design with a wide porch and low floor, making it blend in closely with the surrounding gardens.

Kasumi-dana

The five *keyaki* (zelkova-wood) *Kasumi-dana* (Shelves of Mist) in the Kyakuden hall are artfully designed to resemble a trail of mist. The sliding doors below the bottom shelf are covered in *Yūzen-zomé* printed silk.

The carp painted on the *sugi* (Japanese cedar) panels in the Kyakuden hall are covered in gold netting. This is supposed to stop them from getting out at night and going for a swim in the pond.

JAPANESE GARDENS

Japanese gardens have always tried to represent nature — not slavishly imitating it, but using the limited space available to depict its grandeur, its constant changes, and its wildness. The three main styles of Japanese landscape gardening are the *Tsukiyama*-style, the *Karé-sansui* style (see p. 148), and the *Chaniwa* style (see p. 106). Some gardens, such as those at Shugakuin Imperial Villa, combine the elements of all three styles in the *Tsukiyama* go-round style.

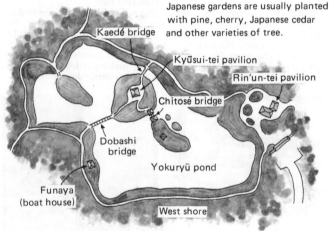

Japanese gardens are usually planted with pine, cherry, Japanese cedar and other varieties of tree.

Kaedé bridge

Kyūsui-tei pavilion

Rin'un-tei pavilion

Chitosé bridge

Dobashi bridge

Funaya (boat house)

Yokuryū pond

West shore

Tsukiyama-go-round-style Gardens

The upper garden of Shugakuin Imperial Villa. The term *Tsukiyama* refers to building up piles of earth to represent mountains. With the addition of streams and ponds representing rivers and lakes, this develops into the grand style of garden known as the *Tsukiyama* go-round style.

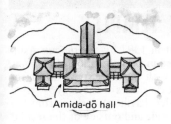

Shinden hall

Amida-dō hall

Jōdo Gardens

At the end of the Heian Era*, a style of garden appeared which attempted to represent a mandala depicting the Buddhist paradise, *Jōdo,* or Pure Land. Such gardens were designed with ponds and islands arranged symmetrically to left and right of a central *Amida** Hall.

Tsukiyama Kanshō-style Gardens

The *kanshō* style of garden is designed to be appreciated from a fixed point such as a building, as opposed to the *kaiyū* (go-round) style, which is admired by walking around it. This type of garden is designed so that its pond and islands and the woods behind them can be viewed at a glance from in front of the Shin-den* (main hall).

Stone lanterns (ishi-tōrō) used in Tsukiyama-style gardens

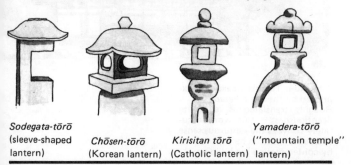

Sodegata-tōrō (sleeve-shaped lantern)

Chōsen-tōrō (Korean lantern)

Kirisitan tōrō (Catholic lantern)

Yamadera-tōrō ("mountain temple" lantern)

●金閣寺
KINKAKU-JI TEMPLE

This three-storied villa was built in 1397 by the *shōgun* Ashi-kaga Yoshimitsu. It is constructed in a combination of *Shinden**, *Buké** and Chinese Zen styles, with the three styles drawn together harmoniously by the delicate curves of the *hōgyō**- style roof. The name *Kinkaku* (Golden Pavilion) derives from the gold leaf used to decorate the inside and outside of the second and third stories. A young priest set fire to the original building in 1950, razing it to the ground, and the present building was constructed in 1955.

Kinkaku-ji Temple's beauty is expressed by the word *basara*.
Roughly translated as "exquisite licentiousness", this word accurately conveys the rapturous sense of beauty that can be experienced by contemplating the building.

Kinkaku in flames

The burning-down of Kinkaku-ji Temple was the theme of Yukio Mishima*'s novel "*Kinkaku-ji*". The young man who set fire to Kinkaku-ji entered the priesthood after becoming entranced with the building's beauty, and gradually became obsessed with the idea that the only thing that could bring his aesthetic senses to perfection would be the sight of the building going up in flames. The novel portrays with stunning power the state of mind of the young priest as he approaches the realization of his vision.

Kyōko pond
The name *Kyōko* means "mirror lake" after the way the pond reflects the villa.

Tsuridono
This fishing pier, which juts out into the Kyōko pond from the west side of the main building, breaks up the otherwise monotonous, square outlines of the villa.

DAITOKU-JI TEMPLE

One of Kyōto's most important temples, Daitoku-ji Temple is the head temple of the *Rinzai-shū* * sect. It was originally constructed in 1319, but most of the present buildings were rebuilt in the 16th century. After Toyotomi Hideyoshi* conducted the funeral of Oda Nobunaga* here in 1582, many *tatchū* (minor temple buildings) were built in memory of various deceased military commanders. Since the tomb of Sen-no-Rikyū is also here, the temple is considered holy ground by all the *chadō** schools, and there are many tea-ceremony rooms and rock gardens.

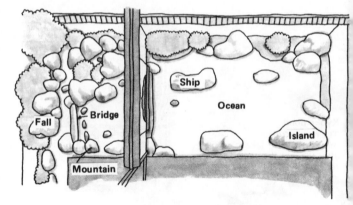

The Hōjō garden of Daisen'in

The rock garden of Daisen'in, one of Daitoku-ji Temple's *tatchū*, is known as a masterpiece of the *karésansui** style. In its confined area of 66 m², skillful use is made of trees, rocks and sand to express the majesty of nature, from waterfalls to valleys and lakes.

Sen-no-Rikyū's tomb is near the Kan'in-seki tea-ceremony room.

Sen-no-Rikyū (1522 – 1591)
This tea master of the Azuchi-Momoyama Era* was the highest authority on *chadō,* the Way of Tea. Departing from existing traditions, he established a new, highly-artistic style of tea ceremony called *wabicha* and became greatly respected. Unfortunately, he drew down upon himself the wrath of Toyotomi Hideyoshi and eventually committed *seppuku* *.

Sen-no-Rikyū's tomb is in the grounds of Jukō-in. The opening in the center of the 2m. high tombstone is to hold sacred fire or an image of Buddha. The tea-ceremony room called Kan'in-seki, which Sen-no-Rikyū designed himself and in which he committed *seppuku,* is also here.

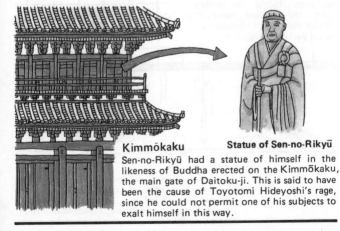

Kimmōkaku

Statue of Sen-no-Rikyū

Sen-no-Rikyū had a statue of himself in the likeness of Buddha erected on the Kimmōkaku, the main gate of Daitoku-ji. This is said to have been the cause of Toyotomi Hideyoshi's rage, since he could not permit one of his subjects to exalt himself in this way.

Ikkyū Sōjun (1394 – 1481)
This eccentric Muromachi-Era* Zen priest developed a philosophy which rejected formalism. He was popular among ordinary people and left numerous legends behind him after his death. The Shinju-an hermitage in Daitoku-ji Temple was built according to his design.

The lower part of the wall of the tea arbor facing the garden is open; this unique construction allows the arbor to become an integral part of the garden.

The entrance to Shinju-an features a *shōji* * which consists of a framework only, allowing cold wind and snow to blow in during winter. It was part of Ikkyū's strict discipline to train the spirit by living under such harsh conditions.

Kohō-an
This *tatchū* was designed by the celebrated 17th-century architect Kobori Enshū as his own personal graveyard. It is famous for its *karé-sansui*-style garden and *Bōsen* * tea-ceremony room.

The fusuma-é* in Shinju-an

Shinju-an contains twenty-nine *suiboku-ga* fusuma* paintings. These priceless paintings, preserved in their entirety, are works of art spanning the period from the Muromachi Era to the Momoyama Era.

The fusuma-é* in Jukō-in

These *suiboku-ga* were painted by Kanō Shōei and his son Eitoku, two of the top artists of the Muromachi Era. The "Plum Tree and Waterfowl" painting is notable for its bold, firm composition based on the thick trunk of the plum tree.

Hosokawa Tadaoki

Kōtō-in

The tomb of Hosokawa Tadaoki* in Kōtō-in was presented to him by Sen-no-Rikyū, who is said to have destroyed the upper part of the tombstone to prevent it from being removed by Toyotomi Hideyoshi. Next to the tomb is that of Hosokawa's wife, Garacia*.

Chadō, the tea ceremony, was extremely popular among the *bushi* (*samurai*) of the Edo and previous eras, and anyone not proficient was looked down on as an uncultured barbarian. The *bushi* therefore spared no expense in obtaining rocks, lanterns, tea-bowls and other objects associated with the tea ceremony and used to convey the spirit of simplicity and quietness known as *wabi*.

CHADŌ(THE TEA CEREMONY)

The tea ceremony, known as *chadō, sadō* or *cha-no-yu,* is a custom in which guests are invited to a special room and served *matcha* (powdered green tea). It is a highly-developed art form with a strict code of etiquette, and it combines the ideals of Zen Buddhism with the uniquely Japanese concept of *wabi.* The design of everything used in a particular school of *chadō* is based on a single, unified philosophy. Participating in the tea ceremony is therefore like entering a separate, self-contained world.

Ceremonial tea-room

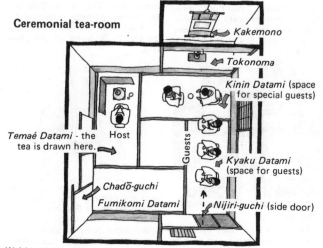

Kakemono

Tokonoma

Kinin Datami (space for special guests)

Temaé Datami - the tea is drawn here.

Host

Guests

Kyaku Datami (space for guests)

Chadō-guchi

Fumikomi Datami

Nijiri-guchi (side door)

Wabi is the avoidance of anything showy or sensuous and the pursuit of simplicity and abstraction. It is the discovery of the true beauty that things possess when stripped of superficial characteristics and reduced to their essence. Even the tea-ceremony room itself is shorn of all superfluity, and a limitless universe is created in an unadorned room with an area of a mere 4 to 8 m^2.

Anyone entering a tea-garden should walk only on the *tobi-ishi* stones.

The guests sit on a bench called *koshikaké-machiai* and wait for the host to call them.

A *naka-mon* (central gate) divides the tea garden into an outer garden *(soto-roji)* and inner garden *(uchi-roji)*. The low gate forces even highly-ranked guests to stoop low, reminding them to discard all thoughts of their worldly status on entering the tea garden.

Ishi-dōrō (stone lantern)

Tsukubai

Since the tea room is regarded as a holy place, guests must cleanse their mouths and hands with water from the *tsukubai*, or stone basin, before entering. The garden is lit at night by the stone lantern behind the *tsukubai*.

Nijiri-guchi

Sekimori

The *nijiri-guchi* is the entrance to the tea-room. The small stone tied with rope is known as a *sekimori*, and its message is "do not proceed beyond this point".

Kakemono

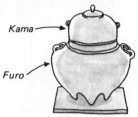

Kama and furo

The *kama* is an iron pot used for boiling the water used to make the tea, while the *furo* is a simple hearth, made of metal or clay, in which charcoal is burnt.

One of the most important of the many art objects and utensils used in the tea ceremony is the *kakemono*, or scroll, hung in the alcove known as the *toko-no-ma*. This is chosen from among Zen-influenced *sho**, *suiboku-ga**, and other works.

Chashaku

A bamboo spoon used to transfer the *matcha* to the tea bowls.

Natsumé

A container for *matcha*

Hishaku

A bamboo ladle used to transfer the hot water from the *kama* into the *chawan*.

Chawan

The *chawan*, or tea bowls, from which the tea is drunk, are of porcelain. Gaily-decorated bowls from China were used originally, but these were gradually replaced by plain, undecorated bowls of Japanese manufacture.

Chasen

The *matcha* and hot water are placed in the bowl and whisked to a froth with the *chasen*, a whisk made from a piece of bamboo split finely and curled over at the ends.

The essence of the tea ceremony is encapsulated in the phrase *"Ichigo Ichié"*. Literally, "one lifetime — one meeting", this phrase expresses the idea that each meeting between host and guests is a unique occasion, never to recur in exactly the same way. The strict rules and formal style of the tea ceremony grew from this idea.

The guests eat cakes while the tea is being prepared.

When the host brings the tea to a guest, the guest should bow.

The guest then draws the tea bowl towards him or herself and says *"Chōdai-shimasu"* (literally, "I receive").

The tea bowl is picked up with the right hand and placed on the palm of the left hand.

The bowl is rotated clockwise approximately 90° in 3 small movements.

The tea is drunk in 3 mouthfuls.

The place where the lips touched the bowl is wiped from left to right between the thumb and forefinger of the right hand, and the fingers are then wiped with special paper carried for the purpose.

The bowl is admired and returned to the host with its front facing the host.

●懐石料理
KAISEKI-RYŌRI

Kaiseki-ryōri is the light meal served before a tea ceremony. Its name derives from *kaiseki*, the term used to describe the stone which a Zen priest under training would place in the front of his robes to give him a feeling of fullness and help him withstand the pangs of hunger. The purpose of eating *kaiseki ryōri* is not so much to enjoy the meal itself but to make it easier to appreciate the subsequent tea ceremony.

Kaiseki ryōri is a plain meal consisting of rice and *"Ichi-jū San-sai"* or "one soup dish and three accompanying dishes".

Hassun
This consists of at least two dishes, usually boiled, one of *umi-no-sachi* (seafood) and one of *yama-no-sachi* (vegetables from the mountains).

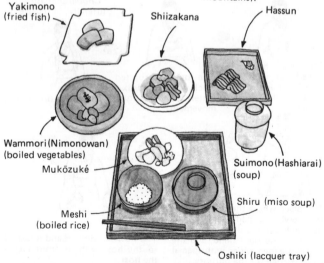

Yakimono
(fried fish)

Shiizakana

Hassun

Wammori(Nimonowan)
(boiled vegetables)

Mukōzuké

Suimono(Hashiarai)
(soup)

Meshi
(boiled rice)

Shiru (miso soup)

Oshiki (lacquer tray)

Kaiseki ryōri forms part of the tea ceremony (the food) which is carefully prepared and elegantly presented but extremely simple; and the associated etiquette is strict. To partake of a *kaiseki* meal used to be considered the height of luxury.

The etiquette at a kaiseki meal

The lids of the *meshiwan* (rice bowl) and *shiruwan* (soup bowl) should be removed simultaneously and placed one on top of the other to the right. The rice should be started first.

The food should not be touched until all the guests have been served.

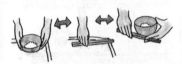

The chopsticks should be placed on the *Oshiki* each time a new dish is picked up.

The *hassun* tray should be picked up and the food admired before eating.

The host serves each guest with *saké* twice. On the second time, the guests should pour *saké* for the host.

After eating, the guests should wipe the dishes with paper and tidy them up.

●上賀茂神社

KAMIGAMO SHRINE

Kamigamo Shrine and Shimogamo Shrine are actually the upper and lower halves of the same shrine, both dedicated to the god Raijin (the god of thunder). Kamigamo Shrine is one of Kyōto's oldest shrines and is said to have existed since the 7th century, before the Heian Era*. The present buildings were all reconstructed from the 17th to 19th centuries, but they are extremely interesting, since they are faithful representations of the ancient style.

Hai-den Hall
Rebuilt in 1628, this building is a rare example of the *Nagaré* * architectural style. The conical heaps of sand in front of the building are for sprinkling on the paths to purify them when a member of the nobility visits the shrine.

This sand would be sprinkled on the paths when important personages came to the shrine to pray.

Karasu-zumō
This children's *sumō* * championship is held on Sep. 9. At the start of the championship, a shrine priest imitates the cry of a crow. This custom is said to have begun when a crow landed on the end of the Emperor's bow in ancient times.

● 下鴨神社

SHIMOGAMO SHRINE

This shrine was built later than Kamigamo Shrine, probably in the middle of the 8th century. Since the time it was built, it has been closely connected with agriculture and has always been of considerable importance. The ancient *shin-den* (shrine buildings) in the *Tadasu-no-Mori* ("forest where lies are revealed"), used as a place of purification, convey an atmosphere of mystery.

Hon-den (Main Hall)

One of Shimogamo Shrine's original regulations was that the main hall should be rebuilt every 20 years. This custom was carried out without a break from 1036 to 1322, after which it was only carried out at irregular intervals. The present building, also in the *Nagaré* style, was constructed in 1629.

Mitarashi-dango

A kind of *dango* (rice dumpling) made specially for the Mitarashi Festival.

Mitarashi Matsuri

In this purification rite, held on the 17th day before *risshū* (the first day of autumn), people wash their feet in the Mitarashi Pond in the shrine grounds. This is said to absolve them of crimes and sins, drive away sickness, and help to ensure safe childbirths.

● 葵まつり

AOI MATSURI

One of the oldest of Kyōto's festivals, held on May 15 every year, the *Aoi Matsuri* has continued since the early part of the Heian Era*. It consists of a procession of people wearing the costume of the Heian aristocracy (see p.82) and proceeds from Kyoto Palace to Shimogamo and Kamigamo Shrines. The name *Aoi Matsuri* (hollyhock festival) is said to come from an order given by a god to "put hollyhocks in your hair and hold a festival for me".

All the participants in the parade adorn themselves with hollyhocks.

Suō — Everyday wear for a *bushi** of the Muromachi Era*.

Suikan — Informal clothes worn by the aristocracy later used as formal wear for children.

The procession consists of four sections. This ox-drawn carriage, called *Gosho-guruma*, is decorated with *aoi* (hollyhocks), *fuji* (wisteria), *shōbu* (irises) and other flowers and appears in the second section.

114

Saiō-no Misogi
A *Saiō* is the unmarried sister of an emperor, offered to a shrine to serve the god of that shrine. The purification of the *Saiō* of Shimogamo Shrine in the river Mitarashi is re-enacted before *Aoi Matsuri*, on May 10.

The last section of the parade consists of women, with the *Saiō* riding in a *kago* (palanquin).

Furyūgasa
Furyūgasa were parasols formerly used by spectators at the festival to shade themselves from the sun.

Mikagé Matsuri
This solemn ceremony, carried out at Shimogamo Shrine before *Aoi Matsuri* on May 12, is held to welcome the gods to the festival proper.

YŪZEN DYEING

This method of dyeing, perfected by the 17th-century Kyōto painter Miyazaki Yūzen, influenced the whole nation with its brilliant colors and novel designs.

The design for a particular color is marked on a paper stencil by perforating the stencil with a needle.

Katazomé Yūzen
In *Katazomé Yūzen,* the dyes are applied through stencils, starting with the palest colors. About twenty different stencils are used for each *kimono.*

Tegaki Yūzen
In *Tegaki Yūzen* (hand-dyed Yūzen), the dyes are applied to each *kimono* individually by hand, using a brush. *Kimono* dyed in this way are the highest class of *Yūzen* product.

The designs used in *Yūzen* dyeing, called *Marutsukushi,* are based on a combination of circular flowers.

●西陣織
NISHIJIN WEAVING

The *Nishijin* weaving method was developed over a thousand years ago in the Imperial Court. Its name is derived from the name of the area of Kyōto where weavers congregated in the latter part of the 15th century. There are many styles of *Nishijin* weaving, but one of the best-known is the *Tsuzuré* style, which has produced many masterpieces such as the tapestries used on the floats in the Gion Festival (see p.64).

Monhori
The pattern data is input into the loom. The processes carried out prior to this step determine the quality of the finished product.

Tebata
High-class products are made on a hand loom *(tebata)*. The unique quality of *Nishijin* weaving is preserved by these skilled craftsmen.

A *Tsuzuré*-weave *kimono*, a fine example of Kyōto elegance.

●延暦寺

ENRYAKU-JI TEMPLE

Saichō* founded Enryaku-ji Temple in 792 after completing seven years of spiritual training as a hermit on Mt. Hiei. The temple became the main temple of the *Tendaishū** sect, while

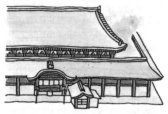

Komponchūdō hall

Rebuilt in 1642, this large hall has a roof constructed in the *Irimoya* style*and features red-painted pillars and galleries. There are many interesting carvings under the eaves of the building, which is an excellent example of a hall in the *Tendaishū* sect style.

The row of flames in front of the altar is said to have been kept alight since the temple was founded over a thousand years ago and is called *"Kiezu-no-Tōmyō"*, or "The light that never goes out".

The Shumidan in Komponchūdō

Enryaku-ji's main hall, Komponchūdō, has a dark and mysterious interior. The *Shumidan* in the center of the hall, an altar on which Buddhist images are placed, features a huge *zushi*, a rectangular chest containing statues of the Buddha and other religious artifacts. This chest houses a Buddha statue carved by Saichō himself.

Mt. Hiei became regarded as a holy place where priests could undergo rigorous training. However, in the 16th century, the mountain and temple became the headquarters of a huge army of priests trained in the military arts. This army began to interfere in politics and aroused the ire of Oda Nobunaga* who attacked the mountain and burned down all the buildings. The temple was not rebuilt until the 17th century.

At the end of the Heian Era*, the age when Enryaku-ji Temple was at the peak of its prosperity, there were about 3,000 *tatchū* (minor temples) on the slopes of Mt. Hiei. Only 3 pagodas and 120 *tatchū* now remain in the three areas known as Tōtō (East Pagoda), Saitō (West Pagoda) and Yokawa.

Jōgyō-dō and Hokké-dō hall in Saitō (West Pagoda Area)

The Emperor's father at that time is famous for saying that "The only things in this world that do not bend to my will are the floods of the river Kamo, the dice in a game of *sugoroku* *, and the *Sōhei*".

Sōhei

In the Sengoku (Warring States) Era*, priests in military uniform, basing themselves at Enryaku-ji Temple and other mountain temples, developed into a powerful force opposing the government. Carrying *mikoshi** and *shimboku** , these warrior priests would descend from their mountain retreats and press their demands on the government by force.

●三千院
SANZEN-IN TEMPLE

Ōhara has been considered since ancient times as a holy place by those who believe in *Jōdo*, the Pure Land or Buddhist heaven. Sanzen-in Temple, built at Ōhara as a residence for the brothers and sisters of deified Emperors, was strongly influenced by this belief. It consists of a beautiful mansion and gardens built in the mountains far from any human habitation. Here the members of the Imperial family would live, praying that they too would become Buddhas after their death.

A plaque bearing the name Sanzen-in.

Ōjō Gokuraku-in

The main hall of Sanzen-in Temple, built in 1148, is dedicated to *Amida** Buddha. The hall's name means "to die and go to heaven." The picture entitled *Bosatsu Raigō*, depicting Bodhisattvas descending from Heaven to save mankind, reflects the *fin-de-siècle* mood of the age.

Seated statues of Amida Nyorai
This rare sculpture is one of the few examples of three Buddhas seated side-by-side. The ceiling, which resembles the hull of a ship, was specially designed to accommodate the large statues.

Oharamé
Oharamé was the name given to the women of Ōhara, who would come into Kyōto bearing on their heads firewood for sale.

Fudō Myō-ō

Guzé Kannon Bosatsu

Butsu-den
The *butsu-den,* (Buddhist statue room) in the *Shin-den* (main hall) houses statues of *Amida Nyorai* in the center, *Guzé Kannon Bosatsu* on the right, and *Fudō Myō-ō* on the left.

KYŌTO ARTS AND CRAFTS

The history of Kyōto's traditional arts and crafts goes back to the Heian Era*, a period of more than a thousand years, and the techniques used to create them, handed down from master to pupil through strict apprenticeship systems, can be seen in all of Kyōto's crafts from objets d'art to everyday goods.

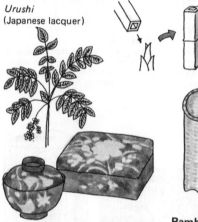

Urushi
(Japanese lacquer)

Kaku-daké
One of Kyōto's specialties is square bamboo, grown by enclosing the growing shoot in a square frame.

bamboo

Kyō-shikki (Kyōto lacquerware)

The techniques for making lacquerware were introduced into Japan from China in the 9th century and perfected by the many highly-skilled *makié-shi* (lacquerware craftsmen) of the Muromachi Era*. Kyōto lacquerware, with its elegant designs and sturdy construction, is regarded as the highest form of this craft.

Bamboo Crafts

The bamboo grown in the Kyōto area is long, glossy and tough; and various techniques for making this fine-quality bamboo into useful or decorative objects were developed many centuries ago. The design of bamboo crafts achieved its highest levels in and after the Momoyama Era*, when bamboo was adopted as a material for making the articles used in the tea ceremony.

Combs and Ornamental Hairpins

The highest-quality combs *(kushi)* are made of *tsugé* (boxwood). Ornamental hairpins *(kanzashi),* which became fashionable in the middle of the Edo Era*, are usually made of tortoiseshell or black-lacquered wood.

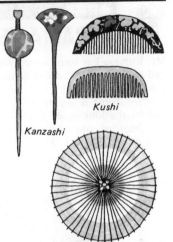

Kushi

Kanzashi

Metal Crafts

Objects made of gold, silver, copper and other metals are used in the tea ceremony or in flower-arranging.

Karakasa (Chinese umbrellas)

These traditional umbrellas are made of thick oiled paper glued onto a framework of split bamboo. The typical pattern seen here is called *ja-no-mé,* or "snake's eye".

Hi-ōgi
(Ōgi without paper)

Ōgi

The *ōgi,* or folding fan, is made of paper glued onto thin bamboo ribs pinned at the base to form a pivot. Various designs are painted on the paper. Originally, *ōgi* were made of a single thin piece of *hinoki* (Japanese cypress) and were written on and used as official documents.

A fan with a typical Kyōto scene depicting the life of the aristocracy in the Heian Era*

123

KURAMA TEMPLE

Mt. Kurama has been feared since ancient times as a haunt of evil spirits and robbers. Kurama Temple, which stands on the side of the mountain, is famous as the place where Minamoto-no-Yoshitsuné is said to have undergone spiritual training with one of the long-nosed goblins known as *Tengu*. The *Kurama-no-Himatsuri*, one of Japan's three biggest "curious festivals", is held here (see p. 173).

Ki-no-Né-Michi
(a path covered in tree roots)

Tengu

Tengu is an imaginary creature which lives in the mountains. It resembles a human being, but has a red face and a long nose.

Minamoto-no-Yoshitsuné

The wars between the two powerful families *Genji** and *Heiké**, which took place in Kyōto in the 12th century, gave rise to numerous tragic events. The tale of Minamoto-no-Yoshitsuné is one of the best-known stories of that era. This young man, who became one of the *Genji*'s military commanders at the age of 25, was blessed with intelligence and good looks, and was skilled in the military arts. He enjoyed great popularity and prestige but was betrayed by his elder brother and eventually committed suicide at the age of 35 after being hunted throughout the country.

JAKKŌ-IN TEMPLE

If Minamoto-no-Yoshitsuné was a tragic hero, the tragic heroine of the age was Kenrei Mon'in, a daughter of the *Heiké* family who was married to the Emperor. Pursued by the *Genji*, she cast herself with her baby prince into the sea but was kept afloat by her long hair and was rescued while her baby drowned. She then cut off her hair, became a nun and went to live in the mountains of Ōhara, in Jakkō-in Temple.

Kenrei Mon'in

The Grave of Kenrei Mon'in
It is said that when Kenrei Mon'in died, purple clouds formed in the west, music was heard, and her room became filled with a mysterious scent.

Kenrei Mon'in is said to have lived in these simple surroundings, chanting daily invocations to Buddha.

125

BUDDHIST TEMPLE ARCHITECTURE

From ancient times until the medieval ages, the most important products of Japanese architecture were Buddhist temples, built to house statues of Buddha and used for the training of Buddhist monks. Just as Buddhism was the basic religion of the country, temple architecture became the basis for all kinds of architecture from shrines to private dwellings and led to the development of various uniquely Japanese designs.

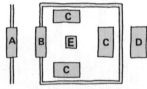

Asuka-dera Style (Asuka Era*)
This type of temple has a pagoda at its center and is bounded by a square cloister.

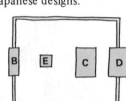

Shitennō-ji Style (Asuka Era*)
All the buildings in this style are arranged in a straight line.

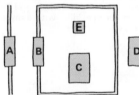

Hōryū-ji Style (Nara Era*)
The pagoda and the *Kon-dō* (main hall) are set side-by-side.

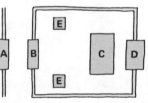

Yakushi-ji Style (Nara Era*)
The main hall is in the center, with two pagodas to the left and right.

The Garan Layout

A Buddhist temple consists of various buildings comprising halls, pagodas and gates. These buildings are known collectively as *garan,* and a number of typical layouts became established for them from the 7th to the 8th century.

A: Nandai-mon gate   B: Chūmon gate C: Kondō D: Kōdō
E: Pagoda

Tōdai-ji Style (Nara Era*)

The pagodas in this type of layout are outside the cloisters.

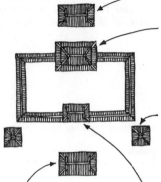

Kōdō
This hall is used for meetings, lectures and discussions.

Kondō
The *kondō*, the main hall of a Buddhist temple, houses the statue of Buddha, the holiest object in the temple. The *kondō* also has other names, such as *hon-dō*, *butsu-den*, *miei-dō*, *amida-dō*, and *komponchū-dō*.

Pagodas
A pagoda is a monument built to house the remains of Buddha, or something representing those remains. Originally, pagodas were the focal point of Buddhist belief, but they gradually took on a more decorative role.

Nandai-mon
A temple usually has four gates facing to east, west, north and south. The biggest of these is the *Nandai-mon*, or South Gate.

Chūmon
The *chūmon*, or Central Gate, is built into the cloister.

Zenshū Style (Kamakura Era*)

This type of layout, introduced from China, has all the buildings arranged in a straight line with no cloister.

Hattō
Kōdō, or assembly hall

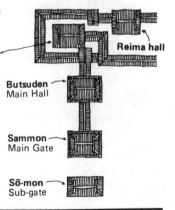

Reima hall

Butsuden
Main Hall

Sammon
Main Gate

Sō-mon
Sub-gate

The change in emphasis in Buddhist temple architecture from the pagoda to the main hall reflects the change in the object of worship from Buddha as represented by the pagoda, to Buddha as represented by various other kinds of images.

Gojū-no-tō (five-storied pagodas) were developed from the Indian stupa, a round shrine originally built to house the remains of Buddha. Crystal or amber is used to represent these remains. The complex structure and mysterious beauty of pagodas places them at the pinnacle of traditional wooden architecture.

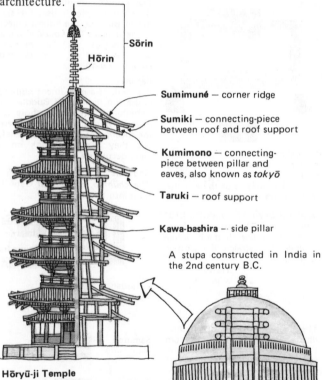

Sōrin

Hōrin

Sumimuné — corner ridge

Sumiki — connecting-piece between roof and roof support

Kumimono — connecting-piece between pillar and eaves, also known as *tokyō*

Taruki — roof support

Kawa-bashira — side pillar

A stupa constructed in India in the 2nd century B.C.

Hōryū-ji Temple
A five-storied pagoda, of height 32 m, built in 617.

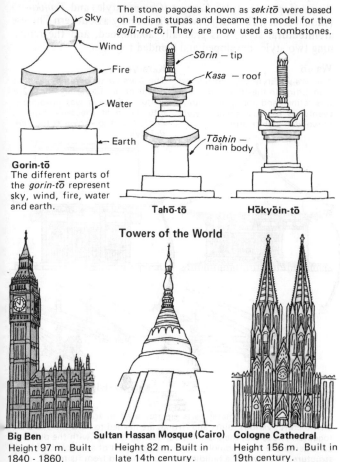

Sekitō

The stone pagodas known as *sekitō* were based on Indian stupas and became the model for the *gojū-no-tō*. They are now used as tombstones.

Sōrin — tip

Kasa — roof

Tōshin — main body

Gorin-tō
The different parts of the *gorin-tō* represent sky, wind, fire, water and earth.

Sky
Wind
Fire
Water
Earth

Tahō-tō

Hōkyōin-tō

Towers of the World

Big Ben
Height 97 m. Built 1840 - 1860.

Sultan Hassan Mosque (Cairo)
Height 82 m. Built in late 14th century.

Cologne Cathedral
Height 156 m. Built in 19th century.

Temple architecture originally consisted of three main types, *Wa-yō* (Japanese style), *Kara-yō* (Chinese style) and *Tenjiku-yō* (Indian style). *Tenjiku-yō*, which is actually a Southern Chinese architectural style, was gradually abandoned, and the remaining two styles developed and blended together.

Wa-yō

The *Wa-yō* style was introduced from China in the 7th century and was refined and improved, leading eventually to Japan's unique style of wooden architecture.

Kara-yō

The *Kara-yō* style resembles that prevalent in China in the 12th century. Since it was introduced into Japan at the same time as *Zen**, it is also known as the *Zen-shū* style.

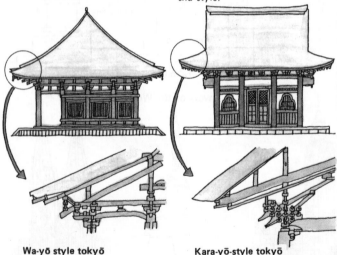

Wa-yō style tokyō

Kara-yō-style tokyō

Tokyō

Since nails or other metal parts are not used in traditional Japanese architecture, various joints and fittings are needed to hold the structure together. The *tokyō*, the assembly connecting the roof with the pillars, is considered the most complex and important part of a temple building's structure. The style of a building can be identified from its *tokyō*.

Pillars

It is also possible to identify the style and period of a building from its pillars.

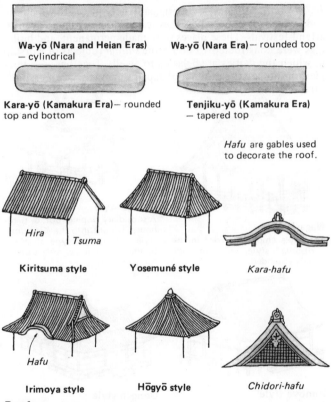

Wa-yō (Nara and Heian Eras) — cylindrical

Wa-yō (Nara Era) — rounded top

Kara-yō (Kamakura Era) — rounded top and bottom

Tenjiku-yō (Kamakura Era) — tapered top

Hafu are gables used to decorate the roof.

Hira   *Tsuma*

Kiritsuma style

Yosemuné style

Kara-hafu

Hafu

Irimoya style

Hōgyō style

Chidori-hafu

Roofs

Roofs are covered with tiles, copper sheet, cypress bark, thatch, boards and other materials, and are constructed in various styles.

131

SHRINE ARCHITECTURE

Jinja (Shintō* shrines) were originally holy places to which the gods would descend when they came down from Heaven to attend festivals. These places were made permanent, and buildings were constructed to house the *shintai* (objects of worship in which the deities are believed to dwell). Together with temples, shrines are the product of Japan's unique style of architecture.

Nagaré style

This style employs a roof in the *Kiritsuma** style, with one side greatly extended.

Kasuga style

A subsidiary sloping roof, or penthouse, is built into the *Kiritsuma*-style roof of this type of shrine building. The prayer area is under this penthouse.

Irimoya style

This is one of the most important styles in shrine architecture, along with the *Nagaré* and *Kasuga* styles.

Gongen style

In this style, the *honden* (main hall) and other buildings are linked together in an H pattern.

Koma-inu

The gates of shrines are guarded by pairs of stone dogs called *koma-inu*. These dogs usually face each other, one with its mouth open and one with its mouth closed.

Un

The one with its mouth open is breathing in and is called *A*, while the one with its mouth closed is breathing out and is called *Un*. The phrase *a-un-no-kokyū*, or "*a-un* breathing" describes a relationship between people so close that they can communicate without words.

A

Torii

The *torii*, or shrine gate, represents a perch for the chickens that used to be sacrificed to the gods.

Chōzuya

Before praying, worshippers purify themselves at the *chōzuya* by washing their hands and rinsing their mouths.

Ring this bell, throw some coins into the offertory box, clap the hands, bow the head, and pray.

Saisen-bako

Money is thrown into the *saisen-bako* (offertory chest) when praying in thanks or supplication.

Kammuri (crown)

Shaku

Hō (over-kimono)

Sashiko (divided skirt)

Asakutsu (shoes)

Kannushi (Chief priest of shrine)

PRIVATE DWELLING

The first Japanese dwellings were pits dug in the ground and covered with straw. After a time, methods of building with wood were introduced from China, and Japanese houses developed over the ages into the type that can be seen today. The houses of the aristocracy and *samurai** of former eras are especially interesting, since they reflect the culture and fashions of the times.

Shōji window

Jōdan-no-ma

Gedan-no-ma (lower hall)

Tatami (rush mats)

A *Shoin*-style residence and an English manor house built at the same period, in the 15th century.

English manor house

Shoin style

This type of dwelling was perfected between the Muromachi and Momoyama Eras. Its name is derived from its similarity to the *sho in* (libraries) of *Zen* temples. Most modern Japanese homes are based on variations of this design.

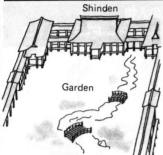

Shinden

Garden

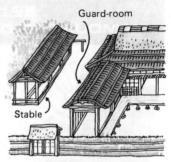

Guard-room

Stable

Shinden style

A typical residence for the Emperors and nobles of the Heian Era*, laid out as three sides of a square, with the *shin-den* (main hall) in the center of the middle side, and a garden with ponds and streams in front.

Buké style

This is the type of house owned by *buké (samurai)* in the Kamakura Era*. With its stables and servants' quarters, it is notable for its unadorned functionality.

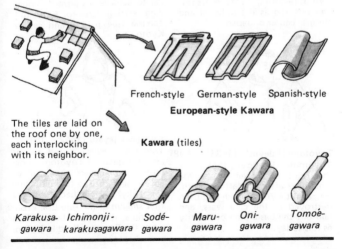

French-style   German-style   Spanish-style

European-style Kawara

The tiles are laid on the roof one by one, each interlocking with its neighbor.

Kawara (tiles)

Karakusa-gawara   Ichimonji-karakusagawara   Sodé-gawara   Maru-gawara   Oni-gawara   Tomoé-gawara

Ashikaga Takauji (1305 — 1358)
The first *Shōgun* * of the Muromachi Era*, Ashikaga Takauji wrested power from the Kamakura Shogunate and removed the seat of government from Kamakura to Kyōto, restoring Kyōto to its former position as the political and cultural center of Japan.

Oda Nobunaga (1534 — 1582)
The weakness of the Muromachi Shogunate had led to a state of civil war in Japan known as the *Sengoku Jidai,* or Warring States Era. Oda Nobunaga put an end to these internal conflicts and reunited Japan. He stopped at nothing to achieve his purpose, including setting fire to Enryaku-ji Temple (see p.118) and central Kyōto.

Toyotomi Hideyoshi (1536 — 1598)
Toyotomi Hideyoshi took over the reins of power from Oda Nobunaga after the latter's death. He rebuilt Kyōto, which had been destroyed in the civil wars, and laid out the basic plan of the city as it is today.

Tokugawa Ieyasu (1542 — 1616)
Tokugawa Ieyasu seized power after the death of Toyotomi Hideyoshi and moved the seat of government to Edo (the old name for Tōkyō), thus becoming the first *shōgun* of the Edo Era. From this time, the *shōgun* lived in Edo while the Emperor lived in Kyōto.

Rakusai, the summer resort
of the nobility in former times, is the
site of many stately old mansions and villas.
Its beautiful natural scenery makes it
one of Kyoto's most popular sightseeing
spots even today.

RAKUSAI

Kyōto prefecture

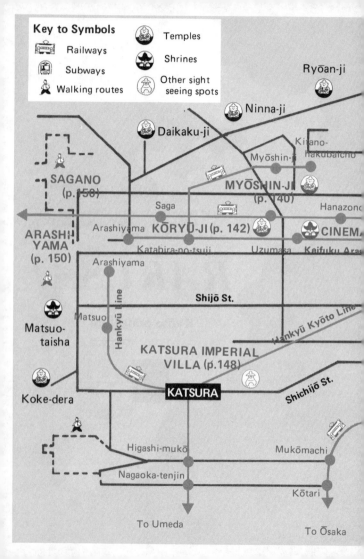

Key to Symbols

- Railways
- Subways
- Walking routes
- Temples
- Shrines
- Other sight seeing spots

Ryōan-ji

Ninna-ji

Daikaku-ji

Kitano-hakubaichō

Myōshin-ji

SAGANO (p.158)

MYŌSHIN-JI (p.140)

Hanazono

Saga

ARASHI YAMA (p.150)

Arashiyama

KORYŪ-JI (p.142)

Katabira-no-tsuji

Uzumasa

Keifuku Aras

CINEMA

Arashiyama

Shijō St.

Matsuo

Hankyū Line

Hankyū Kyōto Line

Matsuo-taisha

KATSURA IMPERIAL VILLA (p.148)

Koke-dera

KATSURA

Shichijō St.

Higashi-mukō

Mukōmachi

Nagaoka-tenjin

Kōtari

To Umeda

To Ōsaka

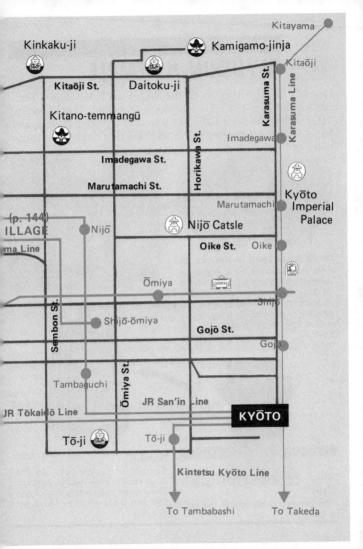

MYŌSHIN-JI TEMPLE

●妙心寺

One of the main temples of the *Rinzai* sect*, Myōshin-ji Temple was built in 1342. Together with Daitoku-ji Temple (see p. 102), it has the most elaborate layout of any *Zen* Temple, and has 43 *tatchū* (sub-temples) in addition to the *sammon* (main gate) and various halls.

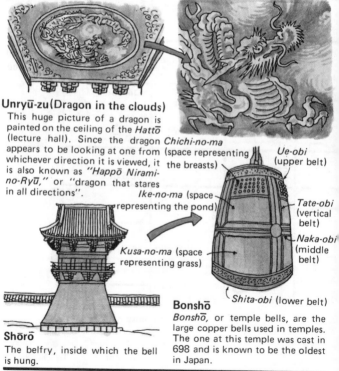

Unryū-zu (Dragon in the clouds)
This huge picture of a dragon is painted on the ceiling of the *Hattō* (lecture hall). Since the dragon appears to be looking at one from whichever direction it is viewed, it is also known as "*Happō Niramino-Ryū*," or "dragon that stares in all directions".

Chichi-no-ma (space representing the breasts)

Ue-obi (upper belt)

Ike-no-ma (space representing the pond)

Tate-obi (vertical belt)

Naka-obi (middle belt)

Kusa-no-ma (space representing grass)

Shita-obi (lower belt)

Shōrō
The belfry, inside which the bell is hung.

Bonshō
Bonshō, or temple bells, are the large copper bells used in temples. The one at this temple was cast in 698 and is known to be the oldest in Japan.

140

The group of Buddhas on the upper floor of the *Sammon*. The ceiling is painted with dragons, heavenly beings and other fabulous creatures in rich colors.

The roof is supported by a complex *tokyō*.

Arrowmarks in the Karamon gate, a reminder of the Warring States Era.

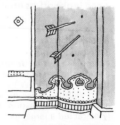

Sammon (Main Gate)

This huge two-storied gate, a masterpiece of Momoyama* architecture, was made in 1599. It is 15 m high.

KŌRYŪ-JI TEMPLE

●広隆寺

Kōryū-ji Temple, built by Shōtoku Taishi* in 603, is one of Japan's oldest temples. The temple buildings were reconstructed in 1165, but most of the Buddha statues that these buildings house were carved in the 7th and 8th centuries.

The *Miroku Bosatsu's* expression is full of variety and gives a distinctly different impression when viewed from a different angle.

Many people have found themselves captivated by the charm of this statue. In 1960, a college student was so overcome by its beauty that he unthinkingly embraced it and broke off its little finger.

This style of crossing the legs is called *hanka*

Miroku Bosatsu

This carving-in-the-round of a *bosatsu** is a fine example of the *Ichiboku** style and ranks among the best of the Buddhist images made in the 7th century. With its crossed legs, its right hand lightly touching its cheek, and its mild and pensive expression, this figure has historically attracted a large number of devotees.

Buddha figures are given many arms so that they can save the souls of many creatures in many different worlds. They are said to have a thousand arms and a thousand eyes, but are usually carved with a standard forty of each.

Double halo

Hana-kammuri (flower crown)

Seat made of white lotus flowers

Juntei Kannon
This Kamakura-Era* painting features a *Kannon** with 3 eyes and 18 arms.

Jūichi-men Senju Kannon
This statue of *Kannon* has 11 faces *(jūichi-men)* and 42 arms. It was carved in the 9th century.

Shōtoku Taishi
This Kamakura-Era carving shows Shōtoku Taishi, who united Japan spiritually under the umbrella of Buddhism at the age of sixteen.

Naki Miroku*
This statue, which appears to be weeping, was given the name "Naki Miroku", or "Crying Miroku".

●東映太秦映画村
TŌEI UZUMASA CINEMA VILLAGE

The Japanese equivalent of the American Western movie is the *jidai geki*, or *samurai** drama, which portrays the adventures of *samurai* rather than cowboys, packing swords instead of pistols. Films for cinema and television are made at Tōei Uzumasa Cinema Village, which is open to the public.

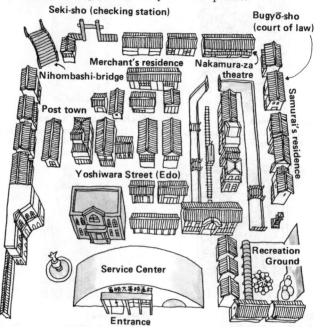

The stage for *jidai geki* is usually set in Edo (old Tōkyō) in the Edo Era*. The Cinema Village has about 20 different types of open-air and indoor sets, most of which are in continuous use.

Kinagashi (loose kimono) -style

The *jutté*, used to trap sword blades in a fight, also served as the *okappiki*'s badge of office.

The *samurai* were the ruling class in the Edo Era, but there were many who, for one reason or another, had no lord to serve and no fixed position. These *rōnin*, or "masterless *samurai*", are the heroes of many *jidai geki*.

Another familiar figure in *jidai geki* is the *okappiki*, or constable, subordinate to the *samurai* responsible for police work.

Yoshiwara
Yoshiwara was the largest red-light district in Edo. This set recreates the scene of a Yoshiwara *yūkaku* (brothel) with its *oiran* (high-class courtesans) and *yūjo* (prostitutes of lesser rank).

Mizu-jaya
The *mizu-jaya* is a teahouse stuffed by young waitresses. Travelers would stop here for refreshment.

● 石庭

ROCK GARDENS

Zen-influenced Japanese-style rock gardens, or *sekitei*, a unique style of garden developed in the Muromachi Era*, employ rocks and white sand to create abstract representations of nature. This style of garden is also called *Karé-sansui*.

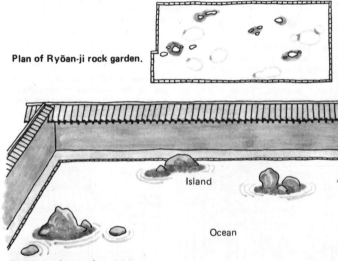

Plan of Ryōan-ji rock garden.

Island

Ocean

The flow of water is represented by white sand

The Rock Garden of Ryōan-ji Temple

One of the most famous of Japan's *sekitei,* this garden consists of a 300-m² area of sand with 15 rocks arranged to represent islands in the ocean. Its high degree of abstractness embodies the ultimate development of the *Karé-sansui* style.

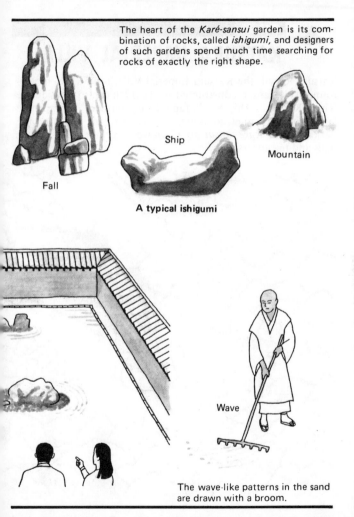

The heart of the *Karé-sansui* garden is its combination of rocks, called *ishigumi*, and designers of such gardens spend much time searching for rocks of exactly the right shape.

Fall

Ship

Mountain

A typical ishigumi

Wave

The wave-like patterns in the sand are drawn with a broom.

KATSURA IMPERIAL VILLA

Katsura Rikyū, the Katsura Imperial Villa, is a 56,000 m² go-round-style garden constructed in the 17th century beside the River Katsura. This world-famous masterpiece of Japanese landscape gardening combines all the different styles of the period, from *Karé-sansui* to *Chaniwa*, together with various halls and tea arbors.

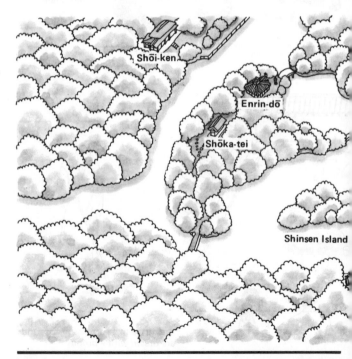

Shōi-ken

Enrin-dō

Shōka-tei

Shinsen Island

*Reservation required

Ama-no-Hashidaté

The low stone bridge which spans the lake just above its surface represents *Ama-no-Hashidaté*.

Ama-no-Hashidaté at Miyatsu Bay in Kyōto Pref., one of the *Nihon Sankei* the three most scenic places in Japan along with Matsushima in Miyagi Pref. and Itsukushima in Hiroshima Pref., consists of a 3-km-long white sandbank covered with pine trees. The *Ama-no-Hashidaté* at Katsura Rikyū is a representation of this.

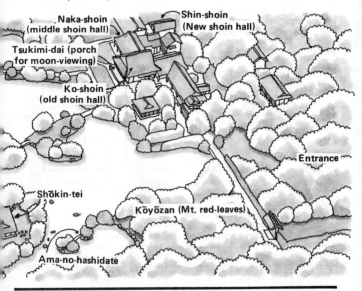

Naka-shoin (middle shoin hall)

Shin-shoin (New shoin hall)

Tsukimi-dai (porch for moon-viewing)

Ko-shoin (old shoin hall)

Entrance

Shōkin-tei

Kōyōzan (Mt. red-leaves)

Ama-no-hashidaté

The gardens and buildings at Katsura Imperial Villa are painstakingly designed, with attention paid to the smallest details.

A door-handle in the shape of a *kasa* (bamboo hat).

This handle is designed to represent pine needles.

The metal fittings with chrysanthemum pattern used on the *chigai-dana* (staggered shelves) in the *shoin* *.

Sankaku-tōrō (triangular lantern).

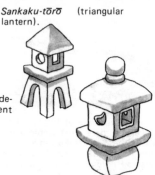

Kirishitan tōro (Catholic lantern). The Latin word FILI is inscribed on the upper part.

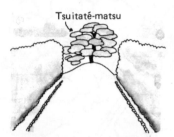

Tsuitaté-matsu

Tsuitaté-matsu
This low pine tree stands at the end of a stone path which extends into the lake, forming a promontory. Since the path is screened on both sides by hedges, a sudden and dramatic view of the lake is obtained from its end.

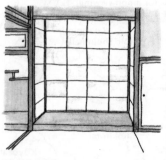

Shōkin-tei
This tea house was used as a villa in summer. The *ichimatsu* (checkerboard) design on the *fusuma* (sliding paper doors) is startlingly vivid even today.

The North Garden seen from the Shōkin-tei
This is considered to be one of Katsura Rikyū's most beautiful views.

Ama-no-hashidaté

Sankaku-dana
(triangular shelf)

Kamado (kitchen range)

World's Famous Gardens

French-style garden
This garden at Versailles Palace was completed in 1715.

Islamic garden
The Alhambra Palace garden, constructed in the 13th century.

ARASHIYAMA AND SAGANO

The area around the Togetsu Bridge, which spans the River Ōi, is called Arashiyama. Its beautiful scenery has been celebrated

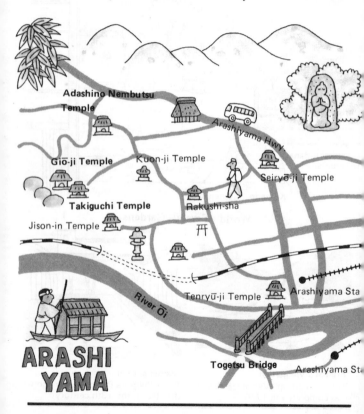

Adashino Nembutsu Temple

Arashiyama Hwy.

Giō-ji Temple

Kuon-ji Temple

Seiryō-ji Temple

Takiguchi Temple

Rakushi-sha

Jison-in Temple

River Ōi

Tenryū-ji Temple

Arashiyama Sta

ARASHI YAMA

Togetsu Bridge

Arashiyama Sta

in poem and song since olden times. The area known as Sagano, which begins on the far side of the bridge, at the base of the mountains, has many temples and villas of the nobility and has witnessed numerous events of historical significance. Arashiyama and Sagano are now two of Kyōto's most interesting sightseeing areas.

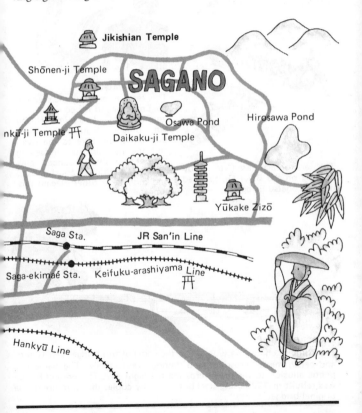

Jikishian Temple
Shōnen-ji Temple
SAGANO
nkū-ji Temple
Daikaku-ji Temple
Ōsawa Pond
Hirosawa Pond
Yūkake Zizō
Saga Sta.
JR San'in Line
Saga-ekimaé Sta.
Keifuku-arashiyama Line
Hankyū Line

Ōgi-nagashi

A pastime in which *ōgi* (fans) are floated down the river.

Mifuné Matsuri

This festival re-enacts the scene of the Emperor and his court boating on the River Ōi. Led by the *Ryūzu-sen* (dragon's-head boat), more than 20 boats take to the river, and the participants, dressed in period costumes, dance, play *gagaku* (traditional court music) and indulge in other elegant pastimes.

The aristocracy used to enjoy boating on the River Ōi, spanned by the Togetsu Bridge.

Togetsu Bridge

The Chinese characters with which the name of this bridge is written, *to* and *getsu,* mean "crossing" and "moon" respectively. The name is a poetic allusion to the moon crossing the night sky. The present bridge was rebuilt in 1934 using steel but faithfully copies the structure of the original bridge.

Many literary works have centered around the Sagano area, and one of the most famous of these is the *Heiké Monogatari*, the tale of the rise and fall of the *Heiké** family. Many tourists still visit the site of the tragic events depicted in this novel.

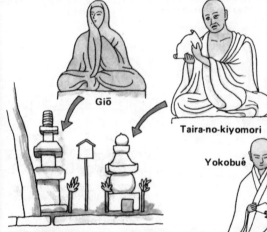

Giō

Taira-no-kiyomori

Yokobué

Giō-ji Temple

The dancer Giō, the lover of the *Heiké* family's supreme commander Taira-no-Kiyomori*, retreated to this temple to live in seclusion after her position had been usurped by another dancer of equivalent rank, Hotoké Gozen. It is said that Hotoké Gozen subsequently realized the futility of her extravagant lift and joined Giō here to spend her days making devotions to Buddha. Giō was 21 and Hotoké Gozen 17 at the time. Their graves are beside the stone pagoda they erected to the memory of Taira-no-Kiyomori on his death.

Takiguchi Temple

One of Taira-no-Kiyomori's officers, Takiguchi Nyūdō, fell in love with a lady by the name of Yokobué. However, there was great opposition to the match, and he retreated to this temple and became a monk. Yokobué discovered his whereabouts and visited him, but was driven away. She then composed a farewell poem and commited suicide.

Adashino Nembutsu Temple

The name Adashino means "place of sadness", and, in olden times, the bodies of those who died without friends or relatives were left here unburied. More than 8,000 stone Buddhas and pagodas have been erected at Nembutsu Temple in prayer for the repose of these dead souls. The scene presented by these Buddhas is said to resemble the dried-up bed of the River Sai, the river that divides this world from Hell.

These stone Buddhas at the entrance to Nembutsu Temple were carved in the Kamakura Era*.

This pagoda at Nembutsu Temple is a copy of the Indian stupa at Santi.

Sentō Kuyō

A memorial service is held at Nembutsu Temple on the evening of Aug. 23rd and 24th, in which lighted candles are placed on the stone effigies. This festival was started to comfort the departed souls of the people whose bodies were laid out at Adashino, since they had no family nor descendants to welcome them when they return to this world for the *bon** festival.

156

A stone Buddha and two-storied pagoda near Ōsawa Pond. Many such scenes can be found when walking on Sagano moor. These stone Buddhas sleeping deep in the forest remind us of the silent prayers of the people of ancient times.

More than 2,000 of the notebooks have been filled.

Jikishian Temple

This temple is famous as a haven for women beset by tangled love-affairs. Many of them have written about their problems in the notebooks kept at the temple, called *Omoidé-gusa,* or "Books of Reminiscences", and some have stayed on and become nuns.

KYŌTO LODGINGS

Kyōto is an internationally-famous sightseeing city, and it has a full complement of hotels and economical *ryokan* (Japanese-style inns). However the lodgings that probably best embody the spirit of Kyōto are the high-class *ryokan*, some with a history of over 300 years. These are built in an elegant combination of the *Shoin** and *Machiya* architectural styles and offer the fabulous service that is a mark of Kyōto hospitality.

Terada-ya

At the end of the Edo Era, Sakamoto Ryōma, patriot of the Tosa clan (Kōchi Pref.) who played a vital part in the Meiji Revolution, was attacked by a group of shogunate assassins while he was staying at this *ryokan*. On this occasion, he countered more than 20 killers firing his pistol. He could barely escape death then.

Tawara-ya

This *ryokan*, praised by the hotel king Conrad Hilton as being the supreme example of devotion to hospitality and selected as one of the world's best eight small hotels by America's Fortune magazine, has become the symbol of Japanese *ryokan*.

Shukubō

Shukubō are *Zen* temples which also offer accommodation. Those staying at these temples are expected to take part in *zazen* (meditation), help with the cleaning, and fit in with the life of the monks.

6:00 a.m. Get up.

6:30 a.m. Listen to a sermon *(hōwa)* from one of the monks and then do *zazen.*

7:30 a.m. Cleaning.

The basic position called "kekka-fuza"

The beginner's position called "hanka-fuza"

ZAZEN

8:00 a.m. Breakfast *(shōjin-ryōri,* see p.74)

The monks are also available for private consultation.

Wagashi — Japanese cakes — are made from various combinations of *mochi* (pounded glutinous rice) and *an* (sweetened azuki bean jam). *Kyōgashi*, cakes made in Kyōto, are considered to be the finest of these. They were originally used in court ceremonies or as offerings to the gods, and the art of making them developed further after they were adopted as part of the tea ceremony.

Toasted Yatsuhashi

Raw Yatsuhashi

Rakugan
Rakugan are dried sweetmeats made by pressing rice flour, *mizuamé* (syrup), sugar and other ingredients in a mold. They are called *rakugan* ("alighting geese") because the black sesame seeds with which they are sprinkled resemble wild geese on a snowfield.

Yatsuhashi
These cakes are made from rice flour baked in the shape of a bridge. There is also an unbaked type called *Nama-yatsuhashi*. The cakes represent a bridge said to have been made by a mother mourning the loss of her child who had been swept away by the river and drowned.

Matsukazé
Matsukazé is a kind of pancake, often used in the tea ceremony, made by baking a mixture of wheat flour, *miso**, sugar and other ingredients.

Tsubaki-mochi
A *mochi* (rice cake) wrapped in *tsubaki* (camellia) leaves.

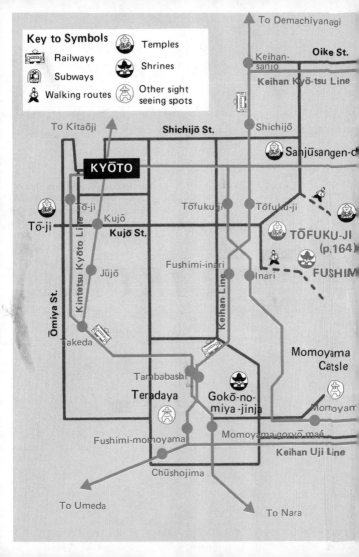

Key to Symbols

Railways
Subways
Walking routes
Temples
Shrines
Other sight seeing spots

To Demachiyanagi
Keihan-sanjo   Oike St.
Keihan Kyō-tsu Line

Shichijō St.
Shichijō
Sanjūsangen-d

KYŌTO

Tō-ji
Tō-ji
Kujō
Tōfuku-ji   Tōfuku-ji
TŌFUKU-JI (p.164)

Kujō St.
Kintetsu Kyōto Line

Jūjō
Fushimi-inari
FUSHIM
Inari
Keihan Line

Ōmiya St.

Takeda

Momoyama Castle

Tambabashi
Teradaya
Gokō-no-miya-jinja
Momoyam

Fushimi-momoyama
Momoyama-goryō maé
Keihan Uji Line

Chūshojima

To Umeda
To Nara

Rakunan, the south side of
the city, is known for the many interesting
temples and shrines dotted along the
railway line linking Kyōto with Nara. It is also
a well-known sake-producing and
tea-growing district.

RAKUNAN

Kyōto prefecture

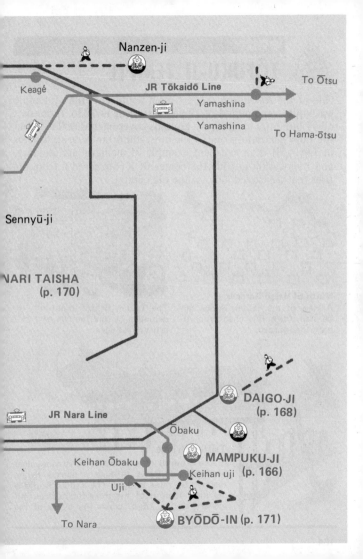

Nanzen-ji

Keage

JR Tōkaidō Line

To Ōtsu

Yamashina

Yamashina

To Hama-ōtsu

Sennyū-ji

NARI TAISHA
(p. 170)

DAIGO-JI
(p. 168)

JR Nara Line

Ōbaku

MAMPUKU-JI
(p. 166)

Keihan Ōbaku

Keihan uji

Uji

To Nara

BYŌDŌ-IN (p. 171)

●東福寺
TŌFUKU-JI TEMPLE

One of the *Rinzai-shū* sect's * main temples, Tōfuku-ji temple was built over a period of 19 years, starting in 1236. It consists of 37 buildings in extensive grounds covering 200,000 m², and the huge *Sammon* is one of the most important *Zen*-style gates in Japan. It is an excellent example of medieval architecture, and its location outside the center of Kyōto saved it from the fires that destroyed most of the old capital.

North of Hassō Gardens
A view of the Tsūten Bridge can be had from this checkerboard-patterned garden.

The Tsūten Bridge in autumn, as depicted by the famous *ukiyoé** artist Hiroshigé.

Tsūten Bridge

In the grounds of the temple, a stream called *Sengyokukan* flows through a narrow ravine spanned by three bridges. The Tsūten Bridge is the most famous of the three for its beautiful scenery during *kōyō,* when the leaves of the trees turn color.

Hyakusai-no-Zō

This statue is said to have been carved by the famous beauty Ono-no-Komachi, who received more protestations of love than raindrops in a storm. It represents how she imagined she would look when she became *hyakusai* (a hundred years old) and shows how she felt on realizing that even her fabulous beauty could not last for ever.

Ono-no-Komachi

Tamazusa Jizō

This statue of Buddha was also commissioned by Ono-no-Komachi. There is an opening in the statue's back, said to hold the amorous missives she received from her legions of admirers.

Tsurukamé-no-Niwa

The rocks in this garden depict a *tsuru* (crane) and a *kamé* (tortoise). When challenged to paint a picture of a tortoise that would move, the *suiboku-ga* (India-ink painting) master Sesshū opted to carve the tortoise in stone, together with a crane, instead of painting it, and the stone tortoise is said to have started moving round the garden at night. Sesshū then rammed a rock through the tortoise's back, pinning it down and preventing it from moving; this is the rock that we see today.

●万福寺
MAMPUKU-JI TEMPLE

Mampuku-ji Temple is a *Zen* temple established in 1661 by the Chinese priest Ingen. It was built in the style of the Chinese Ming Dynasty and is one of the few purely Chinese style temples in Japan.

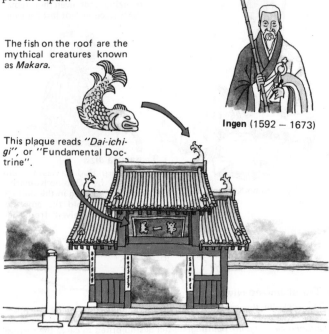

The fish on the roof are the mythical creatures known as *Makara*.

Ingen (1592 – 1673)

This plaque reads *"Dai-ichi-gi"*, or *"Fundamental Doctrine"*.

Sōmon

The stepped roof seen on this gate is the first example of its kind in Japan.

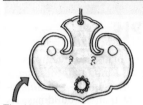

The *Umban* represents a cloud.

The *Kaiban* holds a wooden ball called *Hōju* in its mouth.

The hour is sounded on a wooden fish-shaped drum called *Kaiban*, and meals are announced by striking a copper gong called *Umban*. with a stick.

Jabara Tenjō

Part of the building has no ceiling, exposing the ribs of the roof. This is called *"Jabara-tenjō"*, from its resemblance to the belly of a snake.

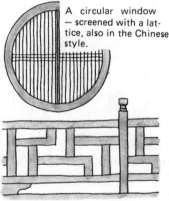

A circular window — screened with a lattice, also in the Chinese style.

A Chinese-style handrail in the corridor constructed from a combination of Buddhist swastikas.

Haku-un-kan

This kind of white-walled gate, painted with Chinese characters, was often used in Chinese castles, but this is the first example of its use in a Japanese temple.

167

●醍醐寺

DAIGO-JI TEMPLE

This temple, established in 926, is one of the main temples of the *Shingon** sect. Built on the side of a mountain, it is separated into two parts; *Kami-Daigo* at the summit and *Shimo-Daigo* at the base; and comprises more than 70 buildings. Its beautiful cherry trees have been celebrated since olden times, and the famous cherry-blossom party *"Daigo-no-Hanami"*, in which Toyotomi Hideyoshi invested a small fortune, took place here.

The low-branched cherry trees at Daigo-ji Temple are famous examples of *Shidaré-zakura* (drooping cherry, or Prunis Pendula).

Toyotomi Hideyoshi

Five-storied Pagoda
Built in 951, this 38 m-high *go-jū-no-tō* (five-storied pagoda) is the oldest in Japan. The *sōrin* (spire) is 13 m tall, and the pagoda houses some excellent Buddha statues and murals.

Hōkō Hanami Gyōretsu
This parade is held every year on the second Sunday of April. The participants, dressed in the costumes of the Momoyama Era, stroll through the grounds of the temple re-enacting the *Daigo-no-Hanami* cherry-blossom party, which took place on March 15, 1598.

168

Daigo Hanami-zu Byōbu

This painted screen depicts the *Daigo-no-Hanami* cherry-blossom party. In order to hold this party, Toyotomi Hideyoshi completely rebuilt the temple, which had been burnt down in the civil wars. This was to be his last great extravaganza, and the whole of the Toyotomi family attended. Two months later, Hideyoshi died, and the Toyotomi family went into decline and eventual eclipse.

Fujito-ishi

This rock is said to have been valued at one thousand *koku* of rice, or the equivalent of about US$500,000. Since it was always in the possession of the ruler of Japan, it was also known as *Ōja-no-Ishi,* or "Rock of Kings". It was moved to the garden of Sampō-in by Toyotomi Hideyoshi.

Sampō-in Temple, regarded as a holy place for the training of priests, is the scene of various forms of spiritual training.

The garden of Sampō-in

Sampō-in Temple is one of Daigo-ji Temple's *tatchū,* or sub-temples. The garden of Sampō-in was laid out by Toyotomi Hideyoshi himself when he had the temple rebuilt.

●伏見稲荷大社
FUSHIMI-INARI SHRINE

Since ancient times, Japanese farmers have believed the fox to be the messenger of the god of harvests, and there are approximately 40,000 shrines in Japan dedicated to this animal. Fushimi-Inari Shrine, which consists of five shrines occupying a large area on the slopes of Mt. Inari, is the most important of the *Inari* shrines and the focus of this popular belief.

Inari
The belief in *Inari,* the fox deity, is a form of animism in which the fox is considered to be a spirit which mediates between the human and the spirit world. In some parts of Japan, a kind of mental illness called *"kitsunetsuki"*, in which a person believes himself to be a fox, is occasionally reported even today, adding a further dimension of mystery to this ancient belief.

Sembon Torii
The approach to the shrine passes through more than 10,000 *torii* (shrine gates) donated by devotees. This unusual scene is the start of a 4 km *"o-yama-meguri"* walking course which takes in all the shrines of Fushimi-Inari.

BYŌDŌ-IN TEMPLE

In the last days of the Heian Era, it was widely believed that *Mappō*, the last days of law and order before the Buddhist Day of Judgement, had arrived. It was thought that after the world had plunged into war, corruption and chaos, 25 *bosatsu** would descend from Heaven to save the world. Byōdō-in Temple, built in the first year of *Mappō* (1052), vividly illustrates the yearning of Buddhists of those days for Gokuraku, the Buddhist Heaven.

Hōō

This mythical Chinese bird is said to appear when a holy king is to be born. It has a front part like that of a *kirin* (Chinese unicorn), a rear part like that of a deer, a head like that of a snake, a tail like that of a fish, a back like that of a turtle, a chin like that of a swallow, and a beak like that of a chicken.

The Hōō-dō can be found on the head of 10 yen coins.

Hōō-dō

The roof of the Hōō-dō, the main hall of Byōdō-in Temple, is decorated with a *hōō,* or Chinese phoenix. The name of the hall derives from the fact that the building itself resembles a *hōō* with its wings outspread. This hall is renowned as one of the most beautiful creations of Eastern architecture.

171

FESTIVALS IN KYŌTO

Kihōraku
This *Setsubun** (bean-throwing) ceremony is held at Rozan-ji Temple on Feb. 3. The participants chase away men dressed as devils by throwing beans at them.

Mibu Kyōgen
This *kyōgen** performance, which teaches Buddhist doctrine through mime, is held every year from Apr. 21 – 29 at Mibu Temple. It is unusual even in Japan.

Yasurai Matsuri
In this festival, held at Imamiya Shrine on the second Sunday in April, men dressed as demons ring bells and beat drums as they dance. The purpose of the dance is to soothe the spirits of flowers and protect people from sickness.

Kamo Kurabé-uma
The horse races known as Kamo kurabé-uma, held at Kamigamo Shrine on May 5, were started in 1093 in prayer for good harvests. The horses race in pairs, with a total of ten races.

Jizō-bon
In this *bon** festival, held on Aug. 23 and 24, children paint stone statues of *Jizō*, the guardian deity of children, and offer cakes and flowers.

Kangetsué
In this *tsukimi** (moon-viewing) festival, held at Daikaku-ji Temple on the night of the full moon in mid-September, the moon is viewed from a boat with a dragon's head on the temple's lake, Ō-sawa-no-Iké.

Zuiki Matsuri
Mikoshi* decorated with agricultural produce appear at this festival, held at Kitano-Temmangū Shrine from Oct. 1 – 5.

Kurama-no-Himatsuri
At this fire festival, held at Kurama Temple on the evening of Oct. 22, young men wearing loincloths parade around the town waving huge 5-m-high *taimatsu* (pine torches).

HISTORICAL TABLE

C.	Era	Japan(Kyōto)	World
6	Asuka Era*	538 Buddhism introduced to Japan	
7		622 Kōryū-ji Temple built (p.142)	622 Islam founded by Mahomet
		678 Kamigamo Shrine built (p.112)	634 Islamic Jihad begins
8	Nara Era*	710 Capital moved to Nara (Heijō-kyō*)	
		711 Fushimi Inari Shrine built (p.170)	711 Saracen army invades Spain
		788 Foundations laid for En-ryaku-ji Temple (p.118)	768 Charlemagne becomes King of the French
	Heian Era*	794 Capital moved to Kyōto (Heian-kyō*)	
		796 Tō-ji Temple built (p.42)	
		Kurama Temple built (p.124)	
		798 Kiyomizu Temple built (p.50)	800 Revival of Byzantine Empire
9		874 Daigo-ji Temple built (p.168)	828 Egbert becomes first King of England
10		876 First Gion Festival held (p.64)	
11		947 Kitano Temmangū Shrine built (p.36)	936 Otto I becomes King of Germany
12		1052 Byōdō-in Temple built (p.171)	
		1164 Sanjūsangen-dō Temple built (p.56)	1096 First Crusade
13	Kama-kura Era*	1192 Kamakura Shogunate established	1189 Innocent III becomes Pope
		1234 Chion'in Temple built (p.71)	
		1243 Tōfuku-ji Temple built (p.164)	
		1272 Foundations laid for Nishi Hongan-ji Temple (p.16)	
		1291 Nanzen-ji Temple built (p.72)	
14		1319 Daitoku-ji Temple built (p.102)	

C.	Era	Japan(Kyōto)	World
	Namboku-chō-Era*	**1331 Emperor moves to Kyōto Palace (p.32)** 1336 Muromachi Shogunate established **1342 Myōshin-ji Temple built (p.140)** **1397 Kinkaku-ji Temple built (p.100)**	1347 Plague sweeps Europe
15	Muro-machi Era*	**1450 Ryōan-ji Temple built (p.146)** 1467−1477 Battle of Ōnin. Kyōto is main battle site. **1482 Ginkaku-ji Temple built (p.84)** **1591 Chishaku-in Temple built (p.70)**	1453 Fall of Byzantine Empire 1480 Ivan 3 lays foundations of Russian Empire 1492 Columbus crosses Atlantic to America
16	Azuchi Momo-yama Era*	**1598 Daigo-no-Hanami (p.168). Hideyoshi dies.** 1600 Battle of Sekigahara **1602 Higashi Hongan-ji Temple built (p.14)**	1522 Magellan circles the globe
17	Edo Era*	1603 Edo Shogunate established. **Nijō Castle built (p.26)** **1620 Katsura Imperial Villa built (p.148)** 1637 Battle of Shimabara* (Christian uprising) 1639 Japan closed to the outside world **1640 Pleasure quarters moved to Shimabara (p.24)** **1641 Shisen-dō Hall built (p.94)** **1655 Shugakuin Imperial Villa built (p.96)** **1661 Mampuku-ji Temple built (p.166)** **1660−1670 Nijō Jinya built (p.30)**	1618 Thirty Years' War begins in Germany 1620 British Pilgrims depart for New World in Mayflower 1649 Cromwell establishes republic in England 1660 English Restoration 1688 The British Revolution
19 20	Meiji Era*	1868 Meiji Restoration 1869 Capital moved to Tōkyō **1895 Heian Shrine built (p.76)** 1904 Japan and Russia at war	1861 American Civil War begins 1914 First World War begins

GLOSSARY

Amidabutsu 阿弥陀仏

The Buddha revered by the Jōdo-shū and Jōdoshin-shū sects. He taught that those who chanted the refrain "Namu-Amidabutsu" would go to the Buddhist heaven after their death.

The Asuka Era (592 — 710) 飛鳥時代

During this era, the capital of Japan was the Asuka district of Nara, and Buddhism was introduced from China and spread throughout the country.

Ashikaga Yoshimasa (1435 — 1490) 足利義政

The 8th *shōgun* of the Muromachi Shogunate, a lover of art and luxury, and devoid of political ability. His weakness led to the Battle of Onin and the eventual downfall of the Muromachi Shogunate.

Bon 盆

The souls of people's ancestors are thought to return to this world at *bon,* the 15th of July by the lunar calendar or the 15th of August by the modern calendar. Various ceremonies are held during the *bon* period; these include *mukaé-bi*, okuribi*,* and *bon-odori (bon* dancing).

Bosatsu 菩薩

A Bodhisattva, or living Buddha (see p.59).

Buké-zukuri 武家造り

A type of residence used by *samurai** in the Kamakura Era*, this simplified version of the Shinden-zukuri* palaces of the nobility became the model for the Shoin-zukuri style* (see p.134).

Bushi 武士

A generic term used to describe the warrior class, or *samurai,* until modern times. Japan was controlled by *bushi* for eight centuries, starting in the 12th century.

Chadō 茶道

The tea ceremony, a code of etiquette used when serving *nihon-cha* (green tea) to guests. Influenced by *zen*,* it attempts to create a world of harmony and tranquillity.

Chaya 茶屋

Originally a tea-house used by travelers for rest and refreshment, the *chaya* developed in Gion into a type of high-class nightclub for the entertainment of Kabuki theater-goers (see p.60).

Chidori Hafu 千鳥破風

A decorative triangular gable built into the sloping roofs of temples and other buildings (see p.131).

Daimyō 大名
A local lord, subject to the authority of the shōgun*.

The Edo Era (1603 — 1867) 江戸時代
An age of great political stability in which Japan was controlled by the shōgun*, starting with Tokugawa Ieyasu*.

The Emperor Kammu (737 — 806) 桓武天皇
The 50th Emperor of Japan. He established Kyōto as the capital in 794 (see p.77).

The Enryaku Era (782 — 806) 延暦時代
The beginning of the Heian Era, when the Emperor Kammu reigned.

Furyū-gasa 風流傘
A long, decorated parasol used when viewing processions and other outdoor events.

Fusuma/Fusuma-é 襖／襖絵
A fusuma is a sliding door made of thick paper on both sides of a wooden frame, used to partition rooms inside a building. The pictures sometimes painted on fusuma are known as fusuma-é.

Geigi 芸妓
A highly-skilled entertainer who sings, dances and plays music at traditional parties. Geigi is the Kyōto name for geisha, and o-chaya-asobi refers to geisha parties held at Kyōto chaya*.

Genji 源氏
The samurai family which founded the Kamakura Shogunate. Famous for its heroic struggle for power with the Heiké family*.

Gongen-zukuri 権現造
One of the styles of shrine architecture developed in the Momoyama Era*, characterized by the layout of the buildings in the form of a letter H (see p.132).

Hayashi 囃子
A type of folk music using fué (flutes), taiko (drums) and shamisen (three-stringed lutes), played mainly at festivals. The Gion-bayashi played at the Gion festival is a particularly famous form of this music.

The Heian Era (794 — 1191) 平安時代

An era when the aristocracy flourished, creating its own refined form of culture, and Kyōto was the capital of Japan.

Heijō-kyō 平城京

The capital of Japan during the Nara Era*.

Heiké 平家

One of the *samurai* families of the 12th century, the Heiké family reached its zenith at the end of the Heian Era, when it gained political control of Japan. However, it lost the struggle with the Genji family, and passed into oblivion after almost all its members had been killed. One of Japan's literary classics is the novel "Heiké Monogatari", which chronicles the family's rise and fall.

Hōgyō-zukuri 宝形造

A type of roof-style in which the roof is square and is decorated with a metal ball called a *hōju* at its peak (see p.131).

Hōnen (1133 – 1212) 法然

Founder of the Jōdo-shū Sect (see p.89).

Hosokawa Tadaoki/Garacia 細川忠興／ガラシャ

One of Oda Nobunaga's generals, Hosokawa Tadaoki (1564 – 1645) was known as a lover of the arts as well as being an intrepid warrior. Unusual for those days, his wife Garacia was a Christian. Regarded as an enemy during the wars for control of Japan, she committed suicide, and, grieving over her death, her husband entered the priesthood.

Hyakunin-Isshu 百人一首

A collection of a hundred poems, each by a different poet. Many such anthologies have been compiled.

Ichiboku-zukuri 一木造り

A method of carving in which a Buddha or other statue is sculpted from a single block of wood (see p. 58).

Irimoya-zukuri 入母屋造り

A type of roof style in which all four sides of the roof are sloped (see p.131)

Ishikawa Goemon (1558 – 1594) 石川五右衛門

This famous 16th-century robber was caught at the age of 37 and sentenced to be boiled to death in a pot together with his infant son. It is said that he desperately tried to save the boy by holding him above the water, not lowering his arms until he was on the point of death. His story became one of the most popular *kabuki* themes.

Jōdo-shū 浄土宗
One of the most important Buddhist sects, founded in the Kamakura Era* (see p.89).

Jōdoshin-shū 浄土真宗
One of the Jōdo-shū* schools (see p.89).

Kabuki 歌舞伎
One of Japan's best-known performing arts, at first performed only by women, but now only by men. It is characterized by its gorgeous costumes, strange makeup and elaborate sets.

Kamakura Era (1192 -- 1333) 鎌倉時代
The era in which the seat of government was located at Kamakura, near present-day Tōkyō. The great *samurai* families, starting with the Genji* family and followed by the Hōjō family, controlled the country during this era, which was also known for its large number of new Buddhist sects.

Kannon 観音
A *Bosatsu** regarded by large numbers of believers as the savior of the world.

Kanō-ha 狩野派
A school of painting founded in the Muromachi Era* and perfected in the Edo Era*, characterized by its rich use of color.

Kara-hafu 唐破風
An arch-shaped gable used to decorate a roof (see p.131).

Karé-sansui 枯山水
A unique type of landscape gardening based on a combination of rocks and sand (see p.146).

Kazunomiya (1846 — 1877) 和宮
Daughter of the Emperor and wife of the *shōgun* of the Edo Shogunate. Famous for her support of the Meiji Restoration*.

Kimono 着物
Japanese traditional dress.

Kiritsuma-zukuri 切妻造り
The most orthodox type of roof style, in which the roof is divided longitudinally by a single central ridge (see p. 131).

Kitano Mandokoro 北政所
The title of the wife of Toyotomi Hideyoshi, famous for her protection of the Toyotomi family after her husband's death.

Kōbō-Daishi 弘法大師

Another name for Kūkai*.

Kūkai (774 — 835) 空海

Founder of the Shingon-shū Sect (see p.88).

Kyōgen 狂言

Kyōgen consists of humorous skits, usually performed during the intervals of a *noh* performance. The genre was established in the Heian Era*.

Maiko 舞妓

Students of *geigi*, these young girls perform traditional dances at *geisha* parties (see p.62).

The Meiji Era (1868 — 1912) 明治時代

In this era, power was restored to the Emperor, the Imperial Palace was moved from Kyōto to Tōkyō, and Japan started to become a modern nation.

The Meiji Restoration 明治維新

At the end of the Edo Era, the Emperor and the *shōgun* fought for ascendancy. The outcome was that power was restored to the Emperor for the first time in eight centuries.

Mikkyō 密教

Mikkyō, or esoteric Buddhism, is one of the two great branches of Buddhism. Its teachings are both mystical and secret, and are not accessible to ordinary people. The Tendai-shū and Shingon-shū sects come under this category. In contrast, Genkyō Buddhism, to which the Jōdo-shū and Jōdoshin-shū sects belong, promotes teachings which are easily understood and are open to anybody.

Mikoshi 神輿

A portable shrine in which a deity is thought to reside during festivals.

Minamoto-no-Yoshitsuné (1159 — 1189) 源義経

A general of the Genji family (see p.124).

Miso 味噌

A brown paste made from fermented soy beans and salt, often used as a seasoning in Japanese cooking.

Miroku 弥勒

A *Bosatsu** who it is believed will appear to save the world 5,670 million years hence.

The Momoyama Era (1582 — 1602) 桃山時代
Japan was ruled by Toyotomi Hideyoshi in this era, the transitional period between the medieval and modern ages. Many superb works of art were produced in this era, which, together with the Heian Era, was one of Kyōto's cultural golden ages.

Mukaebi 迎え火
The fires lit at *bon** to light the way for the souls of people's ancestors as they return to this world.

The Muromachi Era (1392 — 1575) 室町時代
In this era, the strife of the final years of the Kamakura Era was quelled, and Japan was reunited under the Ashikaga family.

Nagaré-zukuri 流造
A type of shrine architecture in which the roofs are designed with one side greatly elongated (see p.132).

The Nara Era (710 — 793) 奈良時代
The era in which Nara was the capital of Japan, an era in which many huge Buddhist temples were constructed.

No/Noh 能
One of Japan's performing arts, in which the players wear masks, and both acting and sets are highly abstract and stylized.

Oda Nobunaga (1534 — 1582) 織田信長
A brave general who survived the Warring States Era* and reunited Japan.

Okuribi 送り火
Fires lit at the end of *bon* to send the souls of people's ancestors back to the spirit world.

Ōmisoka 大晦日
The 31st of December, the last day of the year. On the evening of this day, temple bells are rung 108 times in the custom known as *joya-no-kanê** to cleanse mankind of its 108 sins, and people eat *toshi-koshi-soba* in prayer for long life. In this way, people purify themselves and prepare to face the challenge of the New Year (*Shōgatsu**).

Ōnin-no-Ran/Battle of Ōnin (1467–1477) 応仁の乱
This battle was sparked off by a quarrel over the succession to the title of *shōgun* and developed into a full-scale civil war. Most of the fighting took place in the center of Kyōto, which was almost completely destroyed by fire. The war marked the start of

the Sengoku Jidai* (Warring States Era), when Japan was split up into many local areas ruled by rival barons.

Ono-no-Komachi 小野小町
A poetess and celebrated beauty of the early Heian Era* (see p.165).

Rajōmon 羅城門
The main gate of Heian-kyō and the setting for Kurosawa Akira's film "Rashōmon".

Rinzai-shū 臨済宗
A Zen* sect founded by Eisai in the Kamakura Era*.

Saichō (767 — 822) 最澄
The founder of the Tendai-shū Sect* (see p.88).

Samurai 侍
Another term for *bushi**.

Sansui-ga 山水画
Landscape paintings, one of the three divisions of Eastern painting together with *jimbutsu-ga* (portraits) and *kacho-ga* (paintings of flowers and birds).

The Sengoku Era (1467 — 1581) 戦国時代
The Warring States Era, in which Japan was divided into a large number of separate states. This era came to an end when Japan was reunited by Toyotomi Hideyoshi*.

Senju Kannon 千手観音
A thousand-armed, thousand-eyed *Kannon**.

Seppuku 切腹
Suicide by ritual disembowelment, used as the death penalty for *bushi* in the Edo Era*.

Setsubun 節分
A ceremony held throughout Japan on the 3rd of February, in which people scatter *daizu* (soy beans) around their homes and other buildings to drive out demons and bring in good luck.

The Battle of Shimabara (1637) 島原の乱
An uprising by Christians rebelling against the Edo Shogunate's ban on their religion. Besieged by government troops, they held their castle for a year, but were eventually defeated after many of their members, including women and children, had starved to death.

Shimboku 神木
A holy wooden staff symbolizing a god.

Shinden/Shinden-zukuri 寝殿／寝殿造り
The most popular style of architecture for the residences of the nobility in the Heian Era* (see p.135).

Shingon-shū 真言宗
A Buddhist sect founded in the Heian Era* (see p.88).

Shinran (1173 – 1262) 親鸞
The founder of the Jōdoshin-shū Sect (see p.89).

Shintō 神道
Japan's indigenous religion, akin to animism and deifying the Emperor.

Sho/Shodō 書／書道
The art of calligraphy, in which Chinese characters are painted on *washi* (hand-made paper) with *sumi* (India ink) and *fudé* (brush).

Shōgatsu 正月
New Year's Day, the most important of the year, when various ceremonies are carried out to pray for happiness and prosperity in the year to come.

Shōgun 将軍
In the olden days, this was the highest military rank. It became the usual term for the ruler of Japan when the country changed to a military state in the Kamakura Era.

Shoin/Shoin-zukuri 書院／書院造
A *shoin* is a Japanese-style room used for ceremonies and the entertaining of guests. A type of residence centered around the *shoin,* known as *shoin-zukuri,* became popular in the middle of the Muromachi Era*.

Shōji 障子
A sliding door made by covering one side of a light wooden frame with translucent paper. Used for partitioning rooms and as windows.

Shōtoku-Taishi (574 – 622) 聖徳太子
One of the Emperor's sons, he was the most important political figure of the Asuka Era*. He promoted the unification of Japan by making Buddhism the national religion.

Sōtō-shū 曹洞宗
A Zen sect introduced to Japan from China by the priest Dōgen.

Sugawara Michizané (845 — 903) 菅原道真
A renowned scholar of the early Heian Era (see p.36).

Sugoroku 双六
A traditional dice game in which counters are moved according to the throw of the dice, and the winner is the first to capture his opponent's territory.

Suiboku-ga 水墨画
The painting of pictures in India ink, often used in painting *sansui-ga**.

Sumō 相撲
Traditional Japanese wrestling in which two contestants fight in a circular earthen ring, attempting to push each other out or down.

The Taishō Era (1914 — 1923) 大正時代
A stable period before the outbreak of the Second World War in which French-influenced culture flourished.

Taira-no-Kiyomori (1118 — 1181) 平清盛
The commander-in-chief of the Heiké family's army, he controlled Japan in the last days of the Heian Era. After his death, the Heiké family fell from power.

Tanka 短歌
A form of Japanese poetry akin to the *haiku* but with five lines in a pattern of 5, 7, 5, 7 and 7 syllables.

Tempura てんぷら
A dish in which ingredients such as seafood and vegetables are fried in a light batter. The name is thought to derive from the Portuguese word "tempora".

Tendaishū 天台宗
A Buddhist sect founded in the Heian Era* (see p.88).

The Tokugawa Family 徳川家
The military family which controlled Japan in the Edo Era*.

Tokugawa Ieyasu (1542 — 1616) 徳川家康
The first *shōgun* of the Edo Era, he was a clever politician and astute military commander (see p.136).

Torii 鳥居
The gate of a *shintō* shrine.

Tōrō 灯籠
A square lantern made of stone, bamboo, wood, etc., with translucent paper pasted over the openings.

Tōshō-gū 東照宮
The huge shrine at Nikkō built to the memory of Tokugawa Ieyasu*.

Toyotomi Hideyoshi (1536 — 1598) 豊臣秀吉
The military commander who took over from Oda Nobunaga* in the work of unifying Japan (see p.136,160).

Tsukimi 月見
An elegant pastime practiced by the aristocracy, in which the most beautiful moon of the year, the full moon in September, is viewed from boats on the river.

Tsukiyama 築山
A style of landscape gardening in which earth is piled up to represent mountains (see p.98).

Ukiyoé 浮世絵
Woodblock prints, popular in the Edo Era, depicting landscapes or portraits.

Yosemuné-zukuri 寄棟造
A type of roof style combining four slopes (see p.131).

Yukio Mishima 三島由紀夫
One of Japan's most important modern novelists, Mishima embraced a philosophy which compounded Japanese aesthetics, eroticism, and loyalty to the Emperor. He committed suicide by *seppuku* (ritual disembowelment) on the roof of the Self-Defense Forces headquarters in Tōkyō in 1970. Paul Schrader's film "Mishima", released in 1985, has the novelist as its theme.

Zen/Zen-shū 禅／禅宗
A Buddhist sect which relies on meditation to increase spiritual awareness and achieve enlightenment (see p.89).

Zō-ni 雑煮
A special soup containing *mochi* (rice cakes), eaten at New Year.

INDEX

187

188

S

For Your TraveLife

英文 **日本絵とき事典 5**

ILLUSTRATED
MUST-SEE IN KYOTO

初 版 発 行　1985年9月10日
改 訂 7 版　1991年11月1日
　　　　　　(Nov.1.1991 7th edition)

編 集 人　宮崎　裕
発 行 人　岩田光正
発 行 所　JTB 日本交通公社出版事業局
印 刷 所　交通印刷株式会社

企画・編集　JTB 出版事業局 編集二部
　　　　　　外語図書編集 担当編集長 黒澤明夫
取材・編集協力　株式会社アーバン・トランスレーション
イ ラ ス ト　松下正己
表紙デザイン　東　芳純
翻　　　訳　John Howard Loftus

●図書のご注文は
JTB 出版販売センター　☎03-3477-9588
〒150 東京都渋谷区道玄坂1-10-8 渋谷野村ビル7階
●本書の内容のお問合せは
JTB 出版事業部 編集二部　☎03-3477-9566
〒150 東京都渋谷区道玄坂1-10-8 渋谷野村ビル7階
●広告のお問合せは
JTB 出版事業局 広告課　☎03-3477-9531

913809　712072
ISBN4-533-00528-4